MEDIA AND CONFLICT
ESCALATING EVIL

CEES J. HAMELINK

Copyright © 2011 Paradigm Publishers

Published in the United States by Paradigm Publishers, 2845 Wilderness Place, Suite 200, Boulder, CO 80301 USA.

Paradigm Publishers is the trade name of Birkenkamp & Company, LLC, Dean Birkenkamp, President and Publisher.

Library of Congress Cataloging-in-Publication Data

Hamelink, Cees J., 1940–
    Media and conflict : escalating evil / Cees J. Hamelink.
        p. cm.   (Media and power)
    Includes bibliographical references and index.
    ISBN 978-1-59451-643-6 (hardcover : alk. paper)
    ISBN 978-1-59451-644-3 (pbk. : alk. paper)
    1. Social conflict in mass media. 2. Violence in mass media. 3. Mass media—Political aspects. 4. Mass media—Influence. I. Title.
    P96.S63H36 2010
    303.6—dc22

                                                                      2010014451

Printed and bound in the United States of America on acid-free paper that meets the standards of the American National Standard for Permanence of Paper for Printed Library Materials.

Designed and Typeset by Straight Creek Bookmakers.

15 14 13 12 11   1 2 3 4 5

*To Norman Perryman, great painter of music,
for his artistry and friendship*

CONTENTS

✧

Contents

PREFACE

✧

"War tears, war rends. War rips open, eviscerates. War scorches.
War dismembers. War ruins."

Susan Sontag (2003, February 1)

"Thank you for saving the planet." This note of gratitude is found in
hotel rooms around the world. It asks you to recycle your towels and
makes you feel like a savior. What an enviable simplicity!

Evidently, we should be concerned about the natural environment and
save the drinking water we thoughtlessly use for the laundry. However,
we should be even more concerned with the human-made environment
that may destroy the planet even before melting ice caps and tsunamis
achieve this. We live on a planet with a dangerously aggressive species
whose conflicts can spiral into unimaginable collective destruction.

I did not write this book expecting that it would save the planet;
rather, I wrote it to help understand the "spiral of escalation" and the
role of the mass media in this process. On the basis of a partial understanding of this process (the whole is too complicated for the human
mind to grasp), I propose some ideas on the crucial challenge to de-
escalate conflicts in view of the three most threatening confrontations
in today's world.

Recent uprisings in the Middle East involve a distinctive media dimension, both like and unlike the world has ever seen before. Ongoing

conflicts about the distribution and scarcity of resources, about ethnicity and religion, and about the risks of urban life can easily spiral out of control toward mass slaughter—an evil of huge proportions that is often escalated by the media. At the same time, media can act to bridge gaps and to smooth as well as stir. We need to understand how the "spiral of escalation" works in either direction. How do media create anxiety, provide space for agitation, and disconnect people? How do they bring them together?

Three approaches to the prevention of mass-mediated aggression are proposed in this book: an early warning system for incitement to mass destruction, the invitation to disarming conversations in urban space, and the teaching of "compassionate communication" to children and others. Alertness to the recurrence of collective violence is urgently needed not only in unstable and poor societies but also in established (and emerging) democracies.

Ordinary people can be incited to the mass slaughter of other ordinary people anywhere. Understanding the media's role in this and acting to prevent it are key goals of this book. Looking toward the media's role in bringing people together peacefully (and keeping them together democratically) is the next step.

I was motivated to write this book because, as a European citizen, I am privileged to live in a world region with a great history of enlightenment, humanism, and artistic sophistication. Yet at the same time, I am aware of the numerous atrocities that characterize this European history. In two devastating wars, Europeans killed millions of their fellow citizens. After this explosion of evil, Europeans continued to commit mass murder and torture, both on European soil and elsewhere: the Dutch in Indonesia, the French in Algeria, Stalin in Eastern Europe, fighting parties in the Balkan countries, and the dictatorial regimes of Spain, Portugal, and Greece.

I am deeply concerned about the possibility of twenty-first-century collective political violence in Europe. Could what began after 1945 as a supranational peace project spiral out of control and engage—once again—ordinary European people in political mass murder? Could it happen again?

In the streets of Santiago de Chile, young Chileans chanted "It can't happen here." However, on September 11, 1973, it did happen: A democratic country turned into a violent dictatorship. As Ariel Dorfman noted, one of the most perplexing questions this raises is, "Why did so many of Chile's men and women, heirs to a vigorous democracy, look the other way while the worst sort of abuses were being perpetrated in their name?" (2003, September 29).

Can Europe sit back complacently and consider collective political violence (ranging from illegal detention and deportation to torture, rape, and mass murder) a thing of the past and a phenomenon that belongs to regions with unstable regimes, rampant poverty, and widespread human rights violations?

We have to be careful with singing "It can't happen here" and be alert to the possibility of yet another escalation of human evil. When that does happen again, will we be among the decent and innocent bystanders who allow human dignity to be taken away?

* * *

This book is dedicated to a remarkable artist, Norman Perryman. Over the years, he has painted—with great sensitivity and understanding—the world of music. While working on this book, I was inspired by his representations of Stravinsky's *Firebird*, Yehudi Menuhin performing with Ravi Shankar, the *Misa Criola*, and many other splendid wordless images. Experiencing Perryman's art made me often think of Victor Hugo's observation that music expresses that which cannot be said and on which it is impossible to be silent. It is impossible to be silent on the escalation of evil, and yet one hardly finds any words strong and explicit enough to express one's feelings, fears, and hopes. The portrayal of music by Norman Perryman eventually helped me to find some words to share with the reader.

There are always many people—and among them that special person—who, on the road to the completion of a manuscript, serve as sources of inspiration and guidance. Without providing an extensive list of names, each of these people knows I am grateful for having them around.

Publishing without excellent publishers is a waste of time. The people at Paradigm Publishers (Jennifer Knerr, David Paletz, Martha Whitt, and Josephine Mariea in particular) were an excellent supportive community and contributed much to the clarity and accuracy of the text. Whatever mistakes or obscurities remain are the full responsibility of the author.

—*Cees J. Hamelink, Amsterdam and Marin, France*

INTRODUCTION
CONFLICT AND EVIL

⊷

"The essence of inhumanity is indifference towards our fellow creatures."

George Bernard Shaw

IMAGES OF EVIL

In this book, I struggle with the perennial and troubling question of human evil. Reflecting on the past and future of evil, I try to understand the escalation of human conflict—which is inevitable—into deeds of evil. The search begins with three perplexing images of ordinary people: a Japanese physician, a young German woman, and a Hutu grandmother.

- The Japanese doctor, Nagatomi Hakudo, says in a testimony about his role in the rape of Nanking (1937), "I beheaded people, starved them to death, burned them, and buried them alive, over two hundred in all. It is terrible that I could turn into an animal and do these things. There are really no words to explain what I was doing. I was truly a devil" (Chang, 1997, p. 59). Hakudo participated in one of the many atrocious collective massacres that occurred in the twentieth century. He has no words to explain his violently sadistic behavior.

- The German woman, Frau Vera Wohlauf, a good-looking young woman with a pleasant, open face, has just married captain Julius Wohlauf, the commander of Police Battalion 101. Their honeymoon trip is to Poland. She is pregnant. She attends the mass killings of Polish Jews by her husband's battalion. How could she watch young children being murdered? How could she spend her honeymoon observing how her husband directed genocidal killings that were violent and gruesome?
- The Hutu grandmother takes a wooden stick to beat her Tutsi neighbor's baby to death. How could the violent conflicts between Hutu and Tutsi spiral so out of control that this grandmother became an assassin?

Evil manifests itself in many different forms. In one such manifestation, groups deliberately act to destroy the dignity of fellow human beings. Although this destruction often implies mass slaughter, evil extends beyond the destruction of physical life; it also includes the humiliation of fellow humans. Collective humiliation is a manifestation of evil, as it takes away people's sense of significance and meaning and, thus, amounts to the destruction of their dignity.[1]

In this book I will argue that conflict—both between individuals and between groups—is to a large extent inevitable and can sometimes even be positive and desirable.

The essential moment of concern, however, arises when collective conflict leads to collective evil. Therefore, the following text focuses on the effort to understand when and how this happens. I will seek this understanding in a heuristic way, through exploring the different phases of processes that lead groups of ordinary people from disagreement or uneasiness with other groups of ordinary people to destructive action. In the course of this exploration, I will ask questions about the role of socially mediated constructs such as anxiety and alienation in escalating evil. These questions then lead to the role of the media: are they key agents in social mediation and, therefore, prominent players in collective destructive acting? My preference for a heuristic approach is inspired by a critical warning that the late James D. Halloran gave to his colleagues in the social sciences: "If you ask silly questions, you get silly answers." In his experience, many social studies ended up with largely irrelevant findings because the questions had been wrong in the first place (Hamelink and Linné, 1994). In science, we are often so obsessed with finding answers that we forget we still have to learn how to ask sensible questions.

An important problem that one faces in writing a book on conflict, collective evil, and social mediation is the paucity of research data. We know in fact very little about collective human aggression. The phenomenon of social violence is very complex, so to study it empirically would require longitudinal research and intensive participant observation. Aggression should be studied in situations where it occurs and not in unnatural laboratory settings. However, scientists are usually not present when destructive aggressive incidents occur. Thus, if we want to know more about the biological roots of human aggression, we would have to conduct unacceptable experiments with electric or chemical stimulation, apply lesions to parts of the brain, or deprive human guinea pigs of food and water.

We could use animals instead of human beings. However, animals are studied in controlled laboratory situations that do not reflect reality. And, whatever the findings, can we apply data about animal aggression to humans? Humans are a special species, and in relation to aggression, there are fundamental differences from animals, including the use of language and weapons technology.

Ethological research in the natural habitat of humans or animals would be preferred, but this takes more time and costs more money. If we were to better understand collective destructive action, we would have to conduct a type of forensic ethological investigation in the "killing fields." However, we can only collect data from the reports of survivors and statements by perpetrators during postwar tribunals. Consequently, all the empirical evidence gathered about collective destructive action is limited and largely unreliable.

In addition, there are serious shortcomings in the theoretical conceptualization of collective aggression. We need to gain a better understanding of the sociocultural matrix from which patterns of collective violence emerge.

Recent social research has yielded very useful theoretical analysis of such concepts as risk (in the work of, among others, Beck, Giddens, and Douglas) and trust (in the work of, among others, Etzioni, Giddens, and Luhmann). We still lack comparable work on collective evil. We miss an understanding of how processes in which collective evil escalates are socially mediated and how to position the media in these mediation processes. Understanding the complex interplay among individual emotional experiences; collectively held values, stereotypes, beliefs, and memories (society's collective scripts); and social and infrastructural structures (public spaces and sociocultural institutions like the media) requires the kind of macro-transdisciplinary approach that is not yet on the academic agenda.

It would also seem that most studies on human destructive action focus on individual violence and aggression. Most media and violence studies tend to pertain to individual aggression and to interpersonal violence. Such studies are undoubtedly relevant, but it is more urgent to address the more dangerous social issue of group violence. By now we may know a little about the relationships between media performance and individual violent conduct, but we have no reliable empirical material to help us understand the dynamics between media and collective intergroup conflict.

HUMILIATION

Yet another obstacle on the road to understanding collective evil is the limited knowledge we have about one of the driving forces in the collective destruction of human dignity: humiliation.[2]

New York Times columnist Thomas Friedman (2003) described humiliation as "the single most underestimated force in international relations." We need to not only understand the context and motivations of humiliating behavior but also see that often the perpetrators of violent acts see themselves as victims of humiliation. Those who commit terrorist violence may see themselves as objects of humiliating acts directed against them, their beloved ones, or the group to which they belong. Thus, the experience of humiliation provides a stronger motive for violent confrontations in the world than cultural differences. Humiliation is experienced as an essential loss of personal significance, a loss that needs to be restored. When humiliating acts are targeted against a group, there is a strong motive to regain the lost honor by violent acts such as suicide bombings. The revenge of collective humiliation is meaningful because the group perpetrating it will remember and honor the sacrifice and, thus, restore the lost significance.

Acts of humiliation include:

- De-individualizing people. This means that people's personal identity is undermined; their sense of personal significance is taken away; they are reduced to numbers, cases, or files; and they are treated as group members and not as individuals.

- Discriminating against people such that they are treated according to judgments about superior versus inferior social positions. This means that the "inferior" people are excluded from the social privileges the "superior" people enjoy.
- Disempowering people by denying them "agency." This means that people are treated as if they lack the capacity to make independent choices and actions.
- Degrading people by forcing them into dependent positions in which they efface their own dignity and exhibit servile behavior. In extreme cases, this means frightening people to the point at which they lose control over their physical bodies (dirtying themselves for example) or compelling them to beg on their knees for approval, blessing, or forgiveness.

Acts of humiliation can be used for strategic purposes. In recent wars, the mass rape of women and girls has been used as a weapon against enemies. This represents often a deliberate strategy to humiliate the enemy who cannot protect their own wives, mothers, and daughters. The ultimate humiliation is to impregnate the women of the enemy.

People humiliate each other in interpersonal interactions. This is serious enough, but the bigger problem is those acts of humiliation that are an organic part of institutional behavior—acts that are performed under the authority of an institution (Margalit, 1996, p. 269). Many modern institutions are bureaucratic organizations that, in their mechanical, impersonal way of functioning, provide the space for their employees to commit humiliating acts. We know from social-psychological research (e.g., that of Philip Zimbardo in the well-known Stanford Prison Experiment, 1971) that it is not primarily individual characteristics that motivate people's malicious behavior but rather the situations in which they live and work.[3] Commenting on the humiliating acts by the guards in the Abu Ghraib prison (2006, December 13), Zimbardo said, "in the situation in which the warders had to work this misconduct was practically inevitable." However, those who were politically accountable (among them Defense Secretary Donald Rumsfeld, legal counsel William Haynes, and Vice President Dick Cheney) did not accept their institutional responsibility; instead, it was transferred to the individual warders. This skirting of responsibility is the more abject, as it turns out that the conditions in the prison were deliberately created. A bipartisan report by the Senate Armed Services Committee (December 2008) says that the decisions by the institutional leadership "led directly" to what happened not only in Abu Ghraib but also in Guantánamo Bay and various secret CIA prisons.

In Abu Ghraib, although individuals perpetrated humiliating acts, these individuals also worked under the institutional conditions that made their behavior possible and these same conditions could also have discouraged that conduct. The documentary *Standard Operating Procedure* by Errol Morris demonstrates in detail that the acts by Lynndie England and her colleagues were not merely expressions of sadism (Morris & Gourevitch, 2008). They followed the standard operating procedures that were instituted with the intention to create stressful positions for terrorism suspects. "Aggressive" interrogation methods were sanctioned by the redefinition of torture that was proposed by the U.S. Justice Department and endorsed by Donald Rumsfeld.[4]

It is precisely in extreme situations such as the punishment of criminals that institutions should avoid unnecessary humiliation. There are many illustrations of forms of punishment that are intended to humiliate the convicted. Examples include the Roman crucifixion, the Medieval stake, and the Iraqi gallows. They combine physical pain with mental humiliation. In and of itself, a penitentiary implies a loss of privacy and individual autonomy. This loss, combined with social exclusion, is often humiliating. However, this experience does not render the institutional behavior in itself humiliating. There is an enormous difference between punishment as such and punishment plus deliberate humiliation. The latter may occur in cases in which the warders make no efforts to avoid humiliating acts, such as rapes, among prisoners. The institution also carries responsibility for the humiliating acts committed by its inmates. Performing acts against people's wishes—such as arrests, detention, or security checks—may be unavoidable, but in such situations, there is always the choice for people in charge to treat others with or without humiliation.

There are a number of reasons why acts of humiliation should be rejected. The first is the international human rights commitment to the respect of human dignity. In response to the barbaric acts perpetrated by the Nazis and their allies during World War II, the international community adopted a catalogue of basic values that put respect of "human dignity" center stage. One way to concretize this essential notion of the Universal Declaration of Human Rights (United Nations, 1948b) is to define it as the rejection of all forms of human humiliation. The declaration proposes that people should relate to each other in horizontal, nonhierarchical ways. The first article the declaration states that people are equal in dignity and rights: "All human beings are born free and equal in dignity and rights."

This is the essence of all human rights. In vertical, hierarchical relations, it is a matter of course that the lesser people (slaves, serfs, laborers, women, children) are humble and behave with humility. In those positions, they cannot even be humiliated. This is the prerogative of the privileged classes, who battle with each other (as in duels) to avenge humiliations such as adultery. With the emergence of horizontal networks, however, we can no longer expect that anybody is forced to behave with humility toward others. The human rights' standard of equality implies that all people should expect to be treated in ways that respect their innate dignity. Consequently, institutions with long traditions of vertical relations find it difficult to surrender the privileges of societal hierarchy.

The second argument against humiliation springs from the cross-cultural desire to avoid harm. Throughout the world's religious and ethical systems, we find a powerful motivation to limit human suffering. The motive to avoid otherwise avoidable harm to others and to diminish people's suffering is a key concern in Confucianism, Taoism, Hinduism, Judaism, Christianity, and Islam. Humiliation forces people to undergo avoidable harm. Often people's physical pain is extended into mental pain when, for example, the pain of torture is reinforced by the pain of humiliation. Humiliation is the psychological dimension of human suffering, and the pain caused by humiliation can have consequences that reach far beyond the experience of the physical pain. The physical violence in cases such as rape is, over time, less burdensome than the humiliation of the ultimate submission. This is because the very act of humiliation denies that its victims have value and significance. Thus, humiliation is more than being treated in abusive ways; rather, it is the experience of being seen as having so little dignity that one can be treated by others in abusive ways.

The third argument addresses the historical observation that the experience of humiliation can be manipulated toward violent aggression against others. The classical example is the propagandistic mind management by the Nazi regime in Germany that skillfully transformed the feelings of humiliation among many Germans in response to the Treaty of Versailles, signed on June 28, 1919, into violent resentment against scapegoats such as their Jewish fellow citizens.[5]

CONCLUSION

Scientific exploration cannot be conducted with only one tool, one theory, or one school of thought but instead has to be a flexible, trial-and-error adventure in investigating a problem without the guarantee that a solution will be found or a useful theory will result. The educated guess that guides the present study is that the key components of escalatory processes—the processes that lead humans from dispute to destruction—are socially mediated and that the modern news and entertainment media are the essential vehicles of this mediation. The best we can aspire to in the present investigation is articulated by Herbert Simon's felicitous phrase "satisficing" (Simon, 1957). In other words, we seek solutions that are good enough but could be better. In the following chapters, the exploration of conflict and evil needs to start by reflecting on the nature and development of human conflict.

CHAPTER I

LIVING WITH OTHERS
THE INEVITABLE CONFLICT

✎

"In order to be free one has to reach a measure of independence. However, the complexity of our societies traps human beings in a network of relations that render their independence utterly vulnerable."

Abraham Joshua Heschel (1958)

"Whatever increase in social intelligence and moral goodwill may be achieved in human history, may serve to mitigate the brutalities of social conflict, but they cannot abolish the conflict itself."

Langdon B. Gilkey (2001)

OTHERS AND CONFLICTS

We live with others. We are trapped in networks of mutual dependencies with those others. These relations to others are, according to Freud (1984, p. 98), a source of human suffering that we experience as more grievous than the pain that is caused by the destructive forces of our bodies and nature.

Human existence binds us to each other and, as Sartre wrote (1947), the others can be hell (*"L'enfer c'est les autres"*). In *Huis Clos,* he tells us that to experience living in hell, it is sufficient to spend time with others in an enclosed space. We are strangers to each other, anxious about each other, uncertain about where we are heading and whether we are getting anywhere anyway. We are dependent on each other, and all of us are extremely vulnerable in deep existential ways. We know from the historical record that even in this fragile situation, human beings have a tremendous talent to make hellish life even worse. We have many tricks in our box to make our adversaries into our enemies and to let incompatibilities escalate into violent hostilities.

Living with others is difficult because human interdependence implies that the judgment about who we are—what our significance is—is lodged with others. It is a fundamental feature of human existence that these others are perceived as our adversaries. This perception becomes ever more critical as the communities in which we live—through changes in global demographics—evolve into multicultural and multireligious spaces where we experience increasing density with increasingly more people who are strangers: people of different origin, religious values, cultural practices, and languages. The encounters between "us" and "them" all too often escalate into deadly conflicts. But can these encounters be avoided? Should we ignore each other with "civil inattention" (Goffmann, 1963, p. 84) as many city dwellers do: strangers in the night who avoid eye contact? Or should we opt for living in voluntary "ghettoization" and erect walls between different communities that cannot live in peace? Should we seriously accept the historical possibility that the liberal dream about peaceful, multiethnic, multireligious societies is a dream indeed (Dahrendorf, 2002)?

Human life is impossible without the relations we develop on global, local, and personal levels. These relations are never without conflict. There are always opposing positions, differences, incompatibilities, and disagreements. Conflict is a constitutive element of human life. If we accept this, it seems odd that so much time and energy is invested worldwide in the prevention and resolution of conflict. We should rather direct our efforts to understanding and preventing conflicts from escalating into irreparable damage.

An essential element of the effort to resolve conflict is the Cartesian position that assumes that reality-out-there is a stable given that is cognizable provided we use the correct ways of perception. This means that if our perception is not corrupted by all kinds of societal and personal influences, we can see reality as it is. In order to achieve this objective perception of reality, we need to develop shared values and beliefs. However, as long as people have different values and beliefs, they will see things differently. Thus, it is at this point that the Cartesian position turns out to be a misleading illusion. There is no homogeneity in human perception. In fact, we all live in different universes. Our distinct physiological features and our different personal experiences ensure that we do not live in the same world. Even within the same culture or even the same community, the general experience is that "every man speaks a language somewhat of his own" (Boulding, 1962, p. 295). As a consequence, disagreements and disputes are basic to human existence. Conflict is a central part of living with others. In parent-child relations, it is rare that children and parents do not have different positions. In fact, adolescence is often a time of increased parent-child conflict, when parents and adolescents tend to have different interpretations of the conflict. Parents see disagreements arising from morality, personal safety, and conformity concerns, and adolescents view them as issues of personal choice (Smetana, 1989). What's more, the parent-child conflict does not end at adolescence. Research indicates that many adults continue to have conflicts with their parents. Clarke, Preston, Raskin, and Bengtson (1999) found that intergenerational conflicts can occur regarding styles of interaction, lifestyle choices, child-rearing practices, political and religious values, work habits, and household standards. Thus, conflict is a feature of family life. Sprey (1969, pp. 703–704) noted that families can be viewed as systems in conflict: They consist of "ongoing confrontation between its members, a confrontation between individuals with conflicting interests in their common situation." Relative to other types of relationships, adults report that they experience the greatest degree of criticism and emotional conflict in their marriage, even in happy marriages, followed closely by their relationships with siblings, adolescent children, and parents (Argyle & Furnham, 1983).

Accepting the inevitability of conflict may help us to discover that conflict can even be desirable. Marital conflict may be the best way to discover you made the wrong choice. As Canary, Cupach, and Messman observed (1995, p. 124), "Perhaps more than any other type of interaction, conflict acts as a catalyst for personal development." Even babies learn from the conflicts with their parents how to deal with the conduct of the parental others. As a result, their attempts to resolve these confrontations at all costs may seriously obstruct the independent development of children toward success in reaching maturity.

However, conflict can also be a positive force for change. It can act as an agent of reform, adaptation, and development. Karen Horney (1945, p. 27) stated that "To experience conflicts knowingly, though it may be distressing, can be an invaluable asset." Thus, conflict does not necessarily stand in the way of satisfactory human relations. The frequency of conflict says relatively little about the quality of relationships (Canary, Cupach, & Messman, 1995, p. 126). Instead, conflict can be a source of creativity and growth.

Without conflict, there are no innovations in arts and technology. Without conflict, there can be no science. The basis of scientific investigation is that scientists disagree on almost everything. Thus, when the scientific community claims to have a consensus, one needs to be suspicious about the quality of the scientific work. The claim made by Al Gore and the UN Intergovernmental Panel on Climate Change that the science about global warming is settled is a stunningly unscientific statement. It is inherent to scientific work that there can be no consensus on global warming as the doomsday authorities suggest.

If there had been no confrontations about the validity of theoretical constructs, science would have never moved beyond Aristotelian insights. Scientific progress is a constant process of controversies that lead to the temporary acceptance of paradigms that are then contested by fundamentally new theories and facts. The paradigm that seems better than its competitors will be adopted as the prevailing body of scientific thought until it is contested by even better insights.

Inevitable in the scientific process is that scientists see different things and draw different conclusions even if they make the same observation. Thomas Kuhn gives many telling examples of this in his book on the structure of scientific revolutions (1962).

Without conflict, societies could not be democratically organized. The essence of politics is conflict. Political practice is about the distribution and execution of power and inevitably involves opposite positions. Therefore, disagreement and tension are part of the political process. Expressing these frictions is more productive for democracy than seeking consensus, as consensus politics always tends to exclude people. We have to accept that every consensus exists as a temporary result of a provisional hegemony, as a stabilization of power, and that it always entails some form of exclusion. Pluralist political systems may demand some level of consensual agreement, but this should be a "conflictual consensus" (Mouffe, 2000). A well-functioning democracy calls for a vibrant clash of political positions. Pluralism is inherently an ongoing conflictual process rather than a smooth and rational process. Chantal Mouffe (2000) pleaded for "agonistic" politics, arguing that whereas antagonism is a struggle between enemies, agonism refers to the struggle between adversaries. In politics, there will always be opponents and, thus, conflicts. Particularly among liberal politicians, there is a tendency to obscure this truism, proposing that conflicts can always be resolved through negotiation. Living within a democratic arrangement, however, implies learning to live with fundamental conflicts. The way in which some multicultural societies, like the Netherlands, use the political discourse of "integration" suggest that it is desirable and possible to ignore basic social contradictions and conflicts. This avoidance behavior can be fatal for the development of a strong democracy. In a strong democracy (Barber, 1984), interests and insights will inevitably clash and social conflict never ends.

Conflict is intrinsic to human society and pervades our lives in many different ways, at various levels, and with differing degrees of intensity and various outcomes. This can be described as *a situation in which interdependent human actors engage in verbal or non-verbal disputes about the perceived incompatibility of positions on issues that are relevant to them*. The argumentation for this choice of words runs as follows:

- "Situation" implies the possibility that disputes may be episodic and incidental (fleeting) or permanent and structural.
- The interdependence between actors can be of unequal magnitude and scope. Interdependent relationships can be skewed or balanced in terms of power structure. In the course of interactions, power is essential in the sense of the capacity to set the agenda of a dispute (e.g., by leaving certain issues out) and to influence the outcome of the dispute.
- The reference to perception is pertinent because incompatible positions can be based on delusions or upon empirical observations. The crucial question is whether actors perceive that there are incompatibilities rather than whether these are real.
- Real or imagined incompatibilities can be shallow and of marginal importance or deep and of fundamental significance.
- Issues that people take different positions on cover a wide range and can be almost anything: a claim to ownership of an object, an expectation of affection, a violation of relationship rules, personal preferences, lifestyles, appearances, or modes of communication.

- Positions that actors (individuals, groups, or states) take imply claims to objects of want, which can be material or immaterial and can range from territories to lifestyles, money, love, obedience, or attention. The legitimacy of such claims may be contested by other actors who refuse to comply. Positions may be negotiable because disputes may result from partial information and failed communication. Positions may also be nonnegotiable because the actors are in radical disagreement. If people are in radical disagreement, modes of coexistence must be found that, although they may not resolve the conflict, may tame its escalation toward irreparable damage. After the events of 9/11, many UN member states and religious organizations called for interreligious and intercultural dialogues. The UN 2001 Year of Dialogue between Civilizations put the urgent need for such dialogue on the global political agenda. However, although the proponents of dialogue often assume the readiness to conduct dialogue as a given (Apel, 1988; Habermas, 1993), they ignore the possibility of radical disagreement and irreconcilable differences. Whereas any serious dialogue presupposes that the participants are open to transforming their own prejudices, assertions, and assumptions into questions, those who are locked into their preferred absolutist worldviews are incapable of doing just that.

In both literature and practice, a great deal of attention is paid to preventing and/or resolving conflicts. This attention finds expression in an impressive volume of publications (from scholarly treatises to "for Dummies" pamphlets), an endless series of expensive seminars (with engaging keynote speakers and lavish lunches), and international conferences such as the Deutsche Welle Global Medium Forum in 2008 on "Media in Peacebuilding and Conflict Prevention." All this activity suggests that conflicts can and should be prevented and that they can and should be resolved. However, if indeed conflict is a constitutive element of the human condition and inherent to human life, it cannot be prevented. Moreover, conflicts cannot always be resolved, and sometimes it is even undesirable to want them resolved. Some conflicts are irresolvable because they result from fundamental personality, cultural, or religious differences or from essential and mutually exclusive needs of parties. Conflicts may be insoluble because there is no reasonable answer to the clash of positions. There are situations in life that demand choices between two or more fundamental moral principles that are equally valid but demand different and conflicting courses of action. These are called dilemmas because any course of action violates a basic value. If we violate principle "A" by doing "X," we commit a wrong. Equally, if we violate principle "B" by doing "Y," we also commit a wrong. Thus, we have to decide between two wrongs. The ultimate choice, as presented in the motion picture *Sophie's Choice*, is a confrontation with an insoluble conflict. The movie features Meryl Streep as Sophie, a mother who, in Nazi Germany, faces a choice without a morally satisfying solution when a German soldier gives her the choice to save either her young son or her daughter from deportation and subsequent death. Sophie has to save both her children yet can save only one. No trick from the book can help her to resolve this conflict.

Rather than relying on the conflict resolution gurus, parties should find ways to live with such disputes without irreparably damaging their relationship. People may have disputes about non-negotiable wants that cannot be de-escalated and will have to accept that history just takes its bloody route.

Conflicts have both overt and silent dimensions. If there is no conflict, this may mean the peaceful family is simply between hostilities, in a suspension of warfare. But the mere cessation of hostilities does not mean that a conflict has been resolved. Parties often mull over conflicts long after the confrontational situation has ended, so the silent dispute may continue. Thus, conflicts do not disappear when parties have forgiven each other; they may reappear in different forms. The ending of a conflict may almost immediately lead to another conflict, possibly less violent but still very disturbing for those involved. At the level of family life, an illustration comes from the solution of marital conflicts through divorce, after which the separation may lead the children into conflicts with their parents, their teachers, and other authorities. Although the verbal abuse between the parents is gone, now feelings of guilt and uncertainty afflict the kids and the use of drugs seems the only way out. The core conflict that is caused by a lack of stability and trust in family relations was not resolved.

An illustration at the international level could be the postgenocidal situation in Cambodia. After the unimaginable massacres by Pol Pot and the Khmer Rouge, the liberation arrived, establishing a ruthless "free" market economy that caused enormous gaps between the privileged elite and disenfranchised majorities: a new conflict with its own losers and victims. The core conflict that is caused by the reality of a dangerously divided population was not resolved.

Very real conflicts may be downsized by compromises, but these are not the same as solutions. Compromises often create artificial harmony. Compromise solutions may be accepted even though none of the actors is particularly content with this and the confrontation of positions could—in the end—have yielded a more beneficial outcome (Pruitt & Kim, 2004, p. 97).

Conflicting self-interests between social groups can never be fully resolved. A temporary accommodation may be achieved, usually based upon the physical power that one group is able to wield over the other group. As soon as the other group feels strong enough to challenge this power, however, it will try to change the accommodation toward serving its own collective egoism.

Withdrawing from and avoiding conflict can be constructive in the short term but is often very dysfunctional in the longer term. Real issues and real positions on these issues will not disappear because of avoidance behavior. If one party really wants to address an issue and the other withdraws, this does not lessen the interest the first party has in the dispute and does not improve relational quality.

Often conflicts remain latent and are kept under control by normative rules of conduct that people have formally accepted or internalized for the governance of their behavior in the family, at work, or on the road. Most societies have developed mechanisms to deal with conflict and prevent it from turning violent. Every society has rules, etiquettes, and rituals to cope with conflict in ways that seek to limit the damage done to fellow human beings. In the higher-developed animals, we find a great deal of rituals to avoid such damage. If nonhuman animals kill their own species, they usually kill only a small number. Conversely, human animals are capable of killing vast numbers of their own species in relatively short periods. Thus, human rituals to tame aggression are poorly developed. A partial explanation for this may be that humans throughout history are confronted with strong external disturbances, such as rapid technological developments that create ever-larger distances between points of acting and the consequences thereof. Technology creates "moral distance" between bomber pilots and their victims. In modern warfare, such as in Afghanistan, enemies are killed from great distances: In the Afghan-Pakistan border region, unmanned Predator and Reaper planes are used to fire missiles at enemy targets. Those unmanned aerial vehicles are directed to their targets by Air Force staff in Nevada, United States. Fighters and civilians are destroyed by remote control, and after the killing, the shooters have dinner at home.

The behavior of nonhuman animals that restrains conflict through acts of submission (such as a wolf that offers its bare neck to a stronger contender) may be very rational but tends to be seen by humans as weak behavior. Moreover, human beings are able to kill each other thinking this is what they should do. Humans have an extraordinary capacity of self-justification for extremely cruel behavior.

At the same time, people have also developed ritualizations of aggression and violence that make it possible to compete with others without killing each other. Although sports may illustrate such a ritualization, these activities risk losing their capacity for controlling escalation when professionalization and commercialization transform them into excessive and obsessive competition.

Escalation is difficult to control when there is too much at stake in winning versus losing and when we label the losers as a negative category. In competitive processes, inevitably there are "losers," and our societies are not particularly friendly to those who lose. Recognizing the dignity of the losers is difficult in highly competitive environments.

THE DYNAMICS OF CONFLICT: THE ESCALATION SPIRAL

Martii Ahtisaari, the 2008 Nobel Peace Prize laureate, stated in a press interview, "Every conflict can be resolved" (*International Herald Tribune*, October 11–12, 2008). One can only hope that the interviewer inaccurately quoted the global mediator, as some conflicts cannot be resolved due to the radical disagreement of parties to the dispute. Actually, in most of Ahtisaari's mediation successes, it is likely that conflicts were not fundamentally resolved but instead hostilities were temporarily suspended and may come back with a vengeance.

Some secessionist conflicts ended (e.g., Northern Ireland), but other "old" conflicts erupted again in 2005–2006 (e.g., Sri Lanka). New generations take up old fights, as in Kashmir or in Myanmar. There may be a cease-fire agreement in an ethnic conflict, but the danger of violence remains if this is not yet fully implemented (e.g., Burundi). Or there may be a peace accord in a Muslim-Christian confrontation (e.g., Chad) that is still contested. Hostilities may be over, but parties are ready to resume fighting if final settlements are not achieved or not implemented, as with the Armenians in Azerbaijan, the Kurds in Iraq, and the Dimasas, Garos, Karbis, and Nagas in India. Agreements may be contested, as in the case of the Chittagong Hill Tribes in Bangladesh, the Bougainvilleans in Papua New Guinea, and the Malaitans and Guadalcanalese in the Solomon Islands. In at least fifteen currently active conflicts over self-determination, parties may take up violent tactics again. According to the 2008 Peace and Conflict study,

> in late 2005, for example, violence broke out in Sri Lanka, rupturing a 2002 cease-fire agreement between the government and the Liberation Tigers of Tamil Eelam (LTTE). In Azerbaijan, sporadic clashes broke out over the disputed region of Nagorno-Karabakh, intensifying hostilities that had been relatively quiet for a number of years.... Old adversaries are the most significant source of today's active conflicts.... Most of these conflicts began many years ago. (Hewitt, Wilkenfeld, & Gurr, 2008, p. 23)

The tribal bloodbath in Kenya (2008) is over, but on April 10, 2009, a leading Kenyan newspaper pleaded on its front page: "Don't lead us back to war." All the explosive material for another violent outburst is still in place.

Hewitt, Wilkenfeld, and Gurr refer to this phenomenon as "conflict recurrence." Such terminology suggests that the conflict goes away and then recurs. However, in most of the "conflict recurrences" cited above, the core conflict never stopped; rather, its root causes were not effectively dealt with in conflict mediation efforts (Hewitt et al., 2008, p. 3).

If one concludes that important types of conflict cannot be prevented, cannot really be resolved, and, in some cases, should not be resolved as they are essential to human life and its development, the core problem is not to prevent or to resolve conflicts, but instead to understand the dynamics of conflict. This is particularly important in the serious areas of risk that will be discussed in chapter 6. It is essential to understand how disagreements cross an "invisible line" and develop into lethal confrontations. How do disputes escalate from safety zones to danger zones? Conflicts become dangerous when the invisible line, which has no clear demarcation, is crossed, and there are different invisible lines in different situations. Once they are crossed, conflicts escalate and may have very damaging, even lethal outcomes. Even at festive occasions such as a family Christmas dinner, escalating disputes can be readily observed. Many dinner conversations take the form of disputes, in which opposite positions are expressed. They may end in different ways: They can spiral into violence or finish with a compromise, standoff, stonewalling, or withdrawal. They quickly take a detrimental turn when the tone gets combative. This can happen because of criticizing personal characteristics, making sarcastic remarks, or expressing contempt. A succession of claims and counterclaims in the dispute transforms the family dinner table into a battlefield.

Although human beings have an impressive capacity to cope with serious incompatibilities in creative and constructive ways, sometimes it goes wrong and they move toward destructive aggression. Conflicts may lead parties (nations, groups, individuals) from dispute toward hostility, where the other is no longer an adversary (as in courtrooms or on sports fields) but now an enemy (as in warfare). Escalation implies that incompatible positions move from disputes to violent hostilities—even to warfare. In the process, lighter tools are replaced by heavier tools: Shouting progresses to throwing rocks and then to using firearms. While disputes are escalating, actors shift from looking at an insignificant issue to focusing on an all-encompassing problem with their relationship. They go from arguing to win to the deliberate hurting of the other.

Escalating spirals are often hard to stop once they get started because each side feels that failing to retaliate will be seen as a sign of weakness, inviting further annoying behavior from the other side. In addition, neither side is willing to make conciliatory moves that might break the cycle. One reason for this is that the other is not trusted to reciprocate such assuaging moves: The other is the aggressor and, thus, the one to blame. In the escalation process, the parties become increasingly involved in and committed to the issue at stake.

In escalatory processes, people's environments may provide strong forms of physiological and emotional arousal (Pruitt & Kim, 2004, p. 126), including noise, sexual excitement, alcohol, frustration, anger, time pressure, or air pollution. Such factors diminish the capacity for rational choice making and make people vulnerable to inflammatory encouragements to use violence.

Escalation may be driven by perceptions or experiences of injustice that may originate in events that happened in the past. When victims exaggerate the damage done to them, they are likely to seek revenge. The negative experiences with the adversary strengthen biased perceptions about the other party, and through the mechanism of selective perception, only those characteristics of the adversary that confirm its evil nature are seen. This confirmation justifies hostile attitudes and the use of violence. In the process, the differences between "us" and "them" grow bigger, and interactions between the parties subside, thus giving more space to fake stories, misinformation, and plain lies. Violent action born out of revenge often contributes to a circular process that spirals with every turn into more violence. Once the conflict spirals into the direction of open hostilities, the opponent is—often through propaganda—de-individuated and dehumanized.

In the process of escalation, the cohesiveness of groups tends to become stronger and the readiness to act in extreme ways grows among the individual members of the group. In the escalation process, groups seek strong leaders who are willing to engage in extreme hostile action and to endorse such action. Leaders who come to power because of their forceful and violent performance have an interest in perpetuating the conflict.

In conflict escalation, emotional factors are essential variables, as actors involved in a dispute may want to win their substantial claim but also have fears about losing face or being seen as a loser.[1] In processes of escalation, emotions such as anger, fear, jealousy, grief, greed, shame, sadness, panic, humiliation, or vengeance play a crucial role and have an enormous impact on human behavior. Conflicts are never merely about objective conditions but instead involve subjective feelings. In preventing conflict escalation, focusing on mere substance is insufficient because in disputes, there is both content and context, and the latter is often loaded with emotions. The emotional context may even hinder one from being able to see the rational content of a conflict. For instance, people may be so afraid of terrorism that they are unable to see that terrorists may have substantial and rational political demands. What's more, people's emotional responses to terrorist threats may also obscure that what people perceive as an incomprehensible and sudden outburst of outrage may in fact be the perpetrator's rational response to an undesirable situation. Large-scale murder can be a very rational process executed with conscious intentions and through established organizational structures.

In another example, in the workplace people may have a substantial dispute about getting a salary raise but also worry (the contextual emotion) about not getting this raise. Although the way in which the disputing actors communicate says something about what they substantially want, it also says something about how they feel about each other. In the dispute, a remark by one person of nonconsequential substance may be experienced by another as hostile, thus evoking an antagonistic response that will, in turn, evoke even more hostility.

Because conflicts have both substantive and emotional components, the balance between cognitive capacity and emotional sensitivity is crucial to prevent escalation. When people approach their disputes largely from a cognitive angle and focus on the substance of disagreements, the emotional dimension may get insufficient attention. If they ignore that the conflict may also be about emotions, such as hurt feelings or a sense of betrayal, the rational solution is likely to be temporary only. Alternatively, when the emotional approach fails to discover the rational content of the dispute, the rejection of the (perceived) rationality of demands leads the protagonists into escalation.

It is useful to observe how well in most day-to-day encounters people are capable of maintaining the equilibrium of their cognitive capacity and their emotional sensitivity. This is very fortunate because otherwise we would be permanently involved in civil warfare. However, the risk of escalation is always present, and under certain circumstances, the balance breaks down and disputing parties fail to stop the escalatory process.

People often develop emotional attitudes toward others on the basis of their own actions and, thus, may have hostile attitudes toward those others who they hurt. Such attitudes may endure and escalate because of the human capacity to reduce cognitive dissonance—the discrepancy between what we know (or think we know about ourselves/our self-perceptions) and what we do. We believe we are quite decent and well-tempered people, and yet we scream at others who we see as being the cause of our behavior. Once we establish a negative image of others, we tend to be selective with the information we receive about these people and filter away anything that does not serve our judgment. People are great artists when coping with evidence that undermines their initial impressions. Once the other is seen as evil, whatever he does or does not do only confirms our position. We selectively inform ourselves and selectively evaluate the information. Moreover, we tend to seek information that confirms our position.

Playing on power differences in conflict situations may easily escalate the dispute. Discounting the needs of the weaker actors can cause feelings of humiliation that then lead to hostility and even to violence. When the less powerful perceive that they will lose in the dispute, they may turn to violent action.

As fleeting conflicts shift to low-intensity conflicts, the options for escalation or de-escalation are still open to the actors. When these low-intensity conflicts shift to high-intensity conflicts, the use of violence becomes a realistic option.

The spiral of conflict escalation moves from disagreement through aggression to destruction. The four key drivers of this spiral are: anxiety, agitation, alienation, and accusation in a mirror.

Anxiety[2]

On the basis of historical, social-psychological, and clinical observations, the first phase of the spiral is, arguably, a state of anxiety. I use the concept of anxiety to describe a mixed bag of emotions, including primarily fear, anger, and humiliation. Here, I use anxiety to mean more than simply concern, as there may be nothing wrong with people being concerned about health or climate issues among others. It also indicates more than alertness, as it may be a good thing to be aware of impending dangers. Rather, here I use the concept to denote a condition of "emotional strain" that leads people to feel that they have lost not only control over their lives but also a sense of meaning.

Anxiety is inherent to the human condition. Ontologically, humans live in the permanent tension between Being and Non-Being, between life and death, love and abandonment, success and failure. In a diffuse ("subjective") way, we are aware of uncertainties and threats that are not necessarily connected with "objective" events. We are conscious of gaps between expectation and reality. This existential basic layer finds expression in emotions connected to concrete experiences like illness, unemployment, divorce, or bankruptcy—emotions such as fear, anger, humiliation, shame, and grief.

Although societies have probably always known times of anxiety, a general "state of anxiety" is arguably a prominent feature of modern societies. As opinion polls in European countries, conducted through the Eurobarometer,[3] and in the United States show, people in these countries experience a great deal of anxiety that political, economic, and environmental circumstances will soon get a lot worse. There is a shared anxiety about economics, focusing on inflation, unemployment, and food prices. People are also anxious about the threat of epidemic diseases, credit crises, food shortages, rising prices of oil, terrorism, the danger of Islam, bird flu, genetically modified food, and global warming. Then there is urban anxiety, and its manifestations include locked cars, closed doors, gated communities, and ubiquitous surveillance.

An overall feeling of anxiety means that the world is seen as a dangerous place. This perception has inspired the large-scale manufacturing of surveillance systems, the mushrooming of private security services, and the empty streets at night in many metropolitan centers. Many people are continually anxious about their lives, health, families, relations, money, possessions, or status in society.

Anxiety not only relates to basic human needs such as food, security, and identity, but also to territorial integrity. Like most animals, humans are very concerned about controlling their territory, and they may extend this to include a range of physical objects or even their partners. People are particularly prone to develop these anxieties in competitive environments: Competition breeds anxiety!

Human beings are forever competing, either with one another or with themselves. Competition pervades all human relationships—at work, in school, in the family ("the kids have to win medals in contests") and even in friendships and love. This compulsive competitiveness constrains the human potential for spiritual and moral growth. Its exclusive emphasis on "more, bigger, and better" gives preferential treatment to all those human achievements that can be quantified and, as such, may even constrain human life. Competition aims to extinguish or subjugate one's competitor. Its logical conclusion is the absurdity of leaving no one to compete with: the dictator without people to dictate. But even short of this absurdity, competition leads to irrational behavior, such as crowds competing to get out of a building on fire or a person persistently competing with him/herself and, as a result, becoming a neurotic wreck. Human beings have been competitive throughout history, but necessarily on a limited scale. This competitive nature never mattered so much as it does today. The scale of competition used to be limited because there was only a limited notion of how many potential contenders there were; physical and technical constraints limited the number of competitors that could be eliminated. The environment was perceived as a finite system because the human being was the final point in the evolution and the globe was considered a closed system. Today the scale of competition has dramatically increased because there are more people (population growth), they all want more, and there are more competitors for the same resources. Most physical restraints have been removed in technological development: We can now kill the competitor many times over. The environment is now seen as an infinite system: Competition has no limits and can now also be extended into outer space.

As a result, we are confronted with the unprecedented pervasiveness of competition in practically all social fields. In addition, even our better-intentioned endeavors use such competitive metaphors as "war on poverty," "combat of racism," or "fight against illiteracy." Finally, deceptively as well as perversely, the jargon of economists suggests the ideal of perfect competition. Because our competitive efforts are no longer physically restrained, we need to rely on moral restraint lest we carry our natural instincts to absurd degrees.

Modern capitalism tends to isolate people from each other and creates the lonely, anxious individual as a result of relentless competition (Fromm, 1964). Rollo May suggested that "competitive individualism militates against the experience of community, and that lack of community is a centrally important factor in contemporaneous anxiety" (1977, p. 166). He argued that individualism and the loss of community mean insecurity and a feeling of helplessness (p. 168). This means that in modern capitalism, persons are in fact devalued; we are all for sale. The question "what is my worth?" is a source of constant anxiety, and we persistently worry about success (p. 170). You are worth more if you defeat others—they stand potentially in the way of your success.

Competitiveness implies societal hostility. This hostility leads to more anxiety, which leads to more competition, which leads to more hostility and to more anxiety—and the loop continues.

In many countries where conflicts escalated toward mass violence, there were—before the escalation—states of serious societal anxiety. In Turkey, there was a great deal of anxiety because the Armenians—although for a long time a persecuted and discriminated minority—managed to modernize and make social and economic progress that might in future threaten the Turkish majority. Many Turks felt anxious about threats to Turkish identity as well as feared external aggression (Chalk & Jonassohn, 1990, p. 19). Likewise, there was a general state of anxiety in Germany before World War II, as there was among populations in the Balkan countries before the civil wars. In Rwandan society—before the genocide—Hutus were anxious about what might happen to them in the future, fearing that Tutsis would come to dominate and humiliate them and, as a result, feeling their survival to be threatened. This enabled the political leaders to make people obey their genocidal instructions.

The use of anxiety was very visible as part of the politics of the George W. Bush administration during the post–9/11 period, but it was also exploited in Britain as political instrument. Frank Furedi (2005, p. 126) stated that "Since 9/11, politicians, business, advocacy organizations and special interest groups have sought to further their narrow agendas by manipulating public anxiety about terror." He went on to state that politicians do "regard fear as an important resource for gaining a hearing for their message" (p. 123). Politicians and social movements from different ideological beliefs use people's anxieties to achieve certain goals. He wrote, "political elites, public figures, sections of the media and campaigners are directly culpable for using fear to promote their agenda" (p. 123). Thus, manipulating feelings of helplessness helps to muzzle dissent and calls for unity. This research suggests that in moments of pending disaster, we have to stick together.

Worldwide, environmentalists and health campaigners rouse anxiety. A basic tenet of their scare stories—whether those be about abrupt climate change or genetically modified food—is an alleged and perceived threat that usually is disproportional compared to the real danger. According to Furedi,

> The belief that social solidarity is far more likely to be forged around a reaction to the bad than around the aspiration for the good exercises a strong influence over politicians, opinion makers and academics. Instead of being concerned about the destructive consequences of the mood of anxiety and fear that afflicts the public, many social theorists regard these as sentiments that can be harnessed for the purpose of forging social cohesion. (2005, p. 136)

Sociologists Ulrich Beck (2002) and Anthony Giddens (1994) are among the social theorists who have argued that creating anxiety (particularly fear) functions to positively contribute to societal consensus on crucial issues and to solidarity. Focusing on evil things to come motivates people to act. In fact, Giddens proposed the mobilization of people around a "negative utopia" (1994, p. 223). Fear of the future is idealized as the essential instrument to people's awareness, alertness, and readiness to act. Such visions enjoy wide political and popular support and ignore in a cavalier way that shared anxiety reinforces an in-group identification, the demand for a strong leader, and, thus, exacerbates the fear of the out-group threat that needs to be eliminated. The in-group begins to believe that in order to achieve a good society, the out-group needs to be destroyed. Leaders offer utopian visions that imply the exclusion of the others.

Anxiety increases people's susceptibility to agitation. As a collective state of mind, it makes people vulnerable to manipulation, undermines their autonomous thought and choice, inspires the call for strong leadership, and makes people distrustful of each other. The collective experience of anxiety reinforces group coherence, diminishes and erodes independent thought and autonomous choice, and makes people vulnerable to manipulation, and in their experience of helplessness and uncertainty, the search for strong leadership becomes increasingly important. Anxiety is an unpleasant experience, and the anxious person seeks a scapegoat for his feelings of helplessness and threat. Seeing the world within an "anxiety frame" increases feelings of helplessness, feeds social distrust, and diminishes people's agency (May, 1977, p. 135). For example, in the Balkan conflict, psychiatrists Jovan Raskovic and Radovan Karadzic to a large extent manufactured anxiety about the other. They used the eugenic doctrines developed by German psychiatrists before and during the Holocaust and made them the cornerstones of the politics of "ethnic cleansing."[4] As Raskovic stated, "If I hadn't created this emotional strain in the Serbian people, nothing would have happened" (Citizen's Commission on Human Rights, 2006) Anxiety is a social construction that is probably significantly mediated through a pervasive media discourse about anxiety that has little synchronicity with real-life events.

Agitation

For the second phase of the spiral of escalation, people need to be aroused to collective destructive action. Their anxiety needs to be transformed into aggressive behavior. This requires manipulative leadership. Their anxiety needs the angry political leader (the "capo") who manages to focus the state of anxiety (by identifying the target groups as scapegoats) and who justifies destructive feelings. "Capospeech" is often characterized by inflammatory, divisive, exclusionary, utopian rhetoric, and it is filled with references to past victories or past tragedies (Volkan, 2004, pp. 48–49). In the escalating spiral of the Kosovo conflict, Serb leaders—both political and intellectual—used a historical emotion of martyrdom to incite ordinary Serbs to deeply hate Albanians in Kosovo. Serbs felt societal anxiety because they feared that the expansion of the Albanian Muslim population in Kosovo would outnumber them. Albanians were referred to as a group—and as "terrorists."

Albanians were de-individuated and portrayed as dangerous threats. The leadership propaganda—given a broad public platform in state-controlled Serbian broadcasting—repeatedly suggested that the Serbs were at risk, under threat, and likely to be victims in the near future.

Furthermore, in former Yugoslavia, before the outbreak of the Serb/Croat War, most people felt anxious about the future, a general anxiety that could be manipulated by both Serb and Croat leaders. In their agitation, they used references to historical events and to past injustice to justify and nurture their anxiety. In 1989, at the 600th commemoration of the Battle of Kosovo Polje, Serb leader Slobodan Milosevic assured his followers that Muslims would never again defeat the Serbs, and he referred to deep cultural differences between Serbs and Croats. Alternatively, Croat leader Franjo Tudjman often spoke in his public speeches about the fundamental cultural rift between Croats and Serbs, stating that "Croats belong to a different culture—a different civilization from the Serbs" (Gallagher, 1997, p. 55). Agitation means that the leader expresses anger, identifies the object of anger (the others), and uses inflammatory rhetoric that activates anger and aggression in the followers, who in turn pressure the leader further toward destructive aggression that should lead to the elimination of the object of their anxiety (Volkan, 2004, p. 13). Emphasizing and legitimizing cultural difference makes it easier to target the different others as scapegoats and as the sources of anxiety, whether those different others be Jews (Nazi Germany), peasants (Stalin), people who wear glasses (Cambodia), or the bourgeois (Mao).

The war chant may begin with the "capo," but soon others join the chorus. The capo needs a supportive act—it is never the leader alone! War is not merely a personal initiative but rather a systemic process. Power needs an audience. Imagine that you delete from pictures of agitators such as Adolf Hitler the cheering masses. Power would simply evaporate. What if, in the run-up to the First World War, people had stayed home in Berlin, Paris, St. Petersburg, Vienna and London?

Angry political leaders know how to manipulate people's anxiety to their benefit. They provide a target for people's anger. Hostility needs direction and the leader identifies the targets. He also provides the justification for people's hostile feelings. Essential to this phase of the spiral is that people rally around the leader and collectively create mythical enemies and cleansing rituals. The angry leaders exaggerate people's need to have enemies and lead large groups into a mental regression in which individuality gets lost and collective identity wins over individual identity (Volkan, 2004, p. 159). In this process, basic social trust is replaced with "blind trust" (Volkan, 2004, p. 14). When angry leaders manipulate the sense of collective identity and collective enmity, they prepare the ground for the collective destruction of human dignity.

Alienation

Exposing people to anxiety and agitation does not automatically imply that that they are then ready to humiliate or murder the individual members of the targeted scapegoats. Humans may be a nasty species, but most people do not easily destroy others. Some help is required!

In order to actively or passively participate in collective destructive action, a third phase is essential, in which ordinary people engage in collective humiliation and mass slaughter. This third stage is difficult because even when people are collectively fearsome, angry, and aggressive, they still resist truly and seriously harming other members of the species. Compared to animals, we may kill more easily and more massively, but we should not exaggerate our murderous activities: Most people find it difficult to kill a fellow human being. In most cultures, there are strong taboos against killing the innocent; important moral rules tell people not to kill; and there is the eternal fear of retaliation and punishment. All these factors need to be removed through a process that disinhibits the obstacles to mass murder.

Studies in military history (e.g., Holmes, 1986) suggest that soldiers in combat have often fired over their enemies' heads, and many even did not fire at all. World Wars I and II provide much evidence of soldiers not being able to kill. Dave Grossman (1995, p. 31) stated that "Looking another human being in the eye, making an independent decision to kill him, and watching as he dies due to your action combine to form the single most basic, important, primal, and potentially traumatic occurrence of war." Modern armies focus a great deal of training on techniques of psychological conditioning in order to overcome soldiers' resistance to killing. In these techniques, an essential element is obedience to the leader because very few people kill when they are not ordered to do so: "Many factors are at play on the battlefield, but one of the most powerful is the influence of the leader" (Grossman, 1995, p. 144). Other factors are the role of group pressure (few people kill without the support of their group) and the fear of letting others down (few people can live with the guilt of betraying those with whom one bonded during dangerous situations) (Grossman, 1995, p. 90).

Because only a minority of human beings have no capacity for empathy and cannot feel the pain they cause, the mind management techniques to ease the difficulty of killing are intended primarily to remove empathy by increasing the emotional distance between aggressor and victim. This implies teaching that the victim is inferior, different, and does not deserve the same moral standards as we do. As Helen Fein proposed, through these techniques, the victim is recategorized "outside the universe of moral obligation" (in Benesch, 2004, p. 500). To treat other humans as totally different from us, modern military training requires a process of alienation that disconnects people from one another. Disconnectedness facilitates the de-individuation and dehumanization of the enemy. We are no longer killing human beings but rather demons and animals.

Because effective elimination requires that the object is de-individuated and dehumanized, the perpetrator has to be disconnected from the victim, who is no longer a victim with a face and a unique personality. Human empathy needs to be locked out. This happened, for example, in pre–World War II programs in which the Japanese military trained their troops to kill people who did not attack them. Diary reports of Japanese soldiers reflect the belief that the Chinese were a subhuman species. Thus, the role of dehumanization is likely to be essential in collective violence. Research findings (e.g., the Milgram experiment, 1963) seem to indicate that aggression against an anonymous victim is more likely than against a visible victim.[5]

Accusation in a Mirror

The last decisive step in the spiral of escalation is that the dehumanized others (thought of as cockroaches and vermin) must be seen as real dangers so that killing them can be justified as self-defense. This can be achieved through the reversal of accusations. We accuse them of threatening us. Because most people will kill if their lives are threatened, when they feel their own lives (and those of their loved ones) are endangered if they do not kill the other. When we see the other is guilty of what the aggressor plans to do, he deserves to be punished for intending to exterminate us. Killing then becomes an act of self-defense, and this constitutes—worldwide—the legally and morally acceptable justification for homicide!

CONCLUSION

Life is conflict, and like other animals, people have developed all kinds of rituals to ward off violent confrontations. They are often sufficiently creative in dealing with disputes in constructive—or at least nondestructive—ways. However, quarrels within and between groups can spiral toward forms of collective destructive action and lethal confrontation.

In this escalation of conflict, the first driver is anxiety. This represents a mixed bag of experiences such as fear, anger, grief, humiliation, and shame. Then, for these emotions to become "agents" in the escalation process, they need the drive of external agitation. The "angry" leader exploits these anxious emotions in his inciting rhetoric, and the followers—in a state of arousal—will, in turn, incite the leader to pursue aggressive action. Anxiety and the inclination to solve problems through force are essential to the human condition. If manipulated by unscrupulous leaders, these emotions form a lethal explosive that can transform ordinary people into assassins. The third driver of the spiral encourages people to perceive others as "aliens," as outsiders. Alienation means there is no feeling of solidarity and fellowship: The others are strangers who cannot be trusted; they are members of an out-group who are denied the recognition of their humanity. They are no longer seen as unique individuals, as people like ourselves.

What happens in the escalation process is that the initial difficult problem of serious incompatibility of positions expands and its proportions grow. The adversarial tone becomes hostile as adversaries are increasingly seen as enemies. The tools change from verbal abuse to physical violence. People develop the belief that the enemy (the out-group) must be destroyed and that, eventually, the physical elimination of the enemy will be realized. The aggressor will justify this final deed by reversing accusations: The others posed a lethal threat to our group and we killed them in an act of legitimate self-defense.

These four major drivers in the spiral of escalation are social constructs that, therefore, need to be mediated by social institutions. Among these institutions, the mass media are particularly important channels of mediation. They are the main sources of people's knowledge about conflicts and the key sources of people's frames of thought about conflicts. In the following chapter how far the performance of mass media facilitates the matrix of these four drivers—anxiety, agitation, alienation, and accusation in a mirror—which is basic to the collective destruction of human dignity, needs to be explored.

CHAPTER 2

MEDIA AND THE SPIRAL
OF ESCALATION

⊸⊸

"The mass media are therefore the principal means whereby society is mobilized for killing."

Martin Shaw (2003)

When conflicts are escalating, there is obviously a variety of factors at play, among which are demographic, technological, and economic developments as well as degrees of political motivation and ideological or religious commitment. However, because the essential phases in the escalation spiral are socially mediated largely through the mass media, the key issue for this chapter is the role that media play in the escalation spiral. Media are understood as all those channels through which information, education, and entertainment are disseminated as a public service or a commercial activity to individuals and groups. Such channels include radio and TV programs, newspapers, magazines, films, books, and various Internet vehicles.

Before dealing with the role of media in the escalation of conflict, however, two issues need to be addressed: the "mediatization of conflict" and the interaction between media representations and violent behavior.

MEDIATIZED CONFLICT

The international and national news media bring major conflicts to the world's attention. For most people around the globe, media are the essential information sources about the collective destruction of human dignity.

It is obvious that without news media coverage, we would have little or no knowledge about the hundreds of thousands of victims of massive destruction and aggression in places such as the Congo or Darfur. Without media reports, the victims would be nonexistent for us. This "mediatization" of conflicts (Cottle, 2006) has important consequences for the ways in which media audiences—including leading policy makers—react to such events. This is not without serious problems.

The first problem is that all media reporting is driven by "selective articulation" (Van Ginneken, 1998, p. 16). This means that, inevitably, media providers make choices (e.g., not all conflicts are covered) and emphasize differently according to a convergence of factors, such as political pressures, economic drivers, personal preferences, professional styles, and mechanisms of human perception. Some conflicts are considered more important than others (sometimes the reasons are access, resources, risks, or embeddedness), and in selected conflicts, some parties or dimensions get more attention than others. Thus, selective articulation is inherent in the "media logic," which is the specific way of operating that one finds in most media. Media logic is characterized by the tendency to focus on incidents, accentuate the sensational, dramatize social reality, and decontextualize developments.

Media logic is largely responsible for the prevailing format of conflict reporting: war journalism. Reporting on armed conflict tends to focus on violence and its visible effects, is oriented toward zero-sum thinking, focuses on winners and victories, employs us-versus-them distinctions, and portrays "them as the problem" (Shinar, 2008, p. 9). Dov Shinar (2008, p. 23) went on to note that "Professional values are variables that stimulate the adherence to war journalism." Furthermore, Hackett and Schroeder (2008, p. 26) wrote, "Conventional news routines and news values tend toward conflict escalation." Thus, war news tends to take sides and provides for its consumers little sociopolitical context and historical perspective.

It is inherent to the media logic that media are under a strong pressure to answer the classical five W questions—what, where, when, who, and why—in a single news report. These questions were initially designed to improve objectivity in journalism; however, in real practice they often stand in the way of this objectivity. Although the what, where, and when questions can often be answered without too much difficulty, the trouble arises with the who and why questions. These often require more time, more research, and more prudence. Mainstream journalism has serious problems with these requirements. There is a lot of editorial pressure on journalists to provide answers quickly and with certainty. A great deal of journalism is haunted by an obsession with certainty that often, in all honesty, cannot be provided. Nonetheless, the spin doctors that assist the political leaders in conflicts claim to have all the answers. In the 9/11 attacks, for example, these propagandists knew immediately that the who were Al Qaeda terrorists and the why was hate of American freedoms and lifestyles. This is a tempting offer for news producers and—regrettably—journalists fall easily into the propagandists' traps (Knightley, 2000, p. 496). Thus, as long as journalists do not find the courage to honestly say, "I have no idea," they remain vulnerable to spin doctors' perception management.

During the first Gulf War, journalists around the world reproduced some infamous myths with little or no critical probing. Among these were the Patriot missile success story and the oil spill story. They reported that the Patriot missile had been very effective in intercepting Iraqi Scud missiles launched against Israel. General Norman Schwarzkopf told correspondents this missile was a 100-percent success. Only after the war did the truth emerge: "A U.S. Army Services Committee report quoted in the Guardian of August 17, 1993 concluded, 'A post war review of photographs cannot produce even a single confirmed kill of a Scud missile'" (Knightley, 2000, p. 496). In a testimony before the House Armed Services Committee, former Defense Department official Pierre Sprey stated, "The country has been poorly served by shamelessly doctored statistics and the hand-selected video clips of isolated successes that were pumped out to the media during the war in order to influence post-war budget decisions" (Knightley, 2000, p. 497). Most war correspondents were "pretty impressively ignorant about technology" (Knightley, 2000, p. 497) and acted as unpaid publicists in order to help weapons manufacturers get government contracts.

In the second example, the image of the dying cormorant choked by an oil slick that the Iraqis had released from Kuwait portrayed Saddam Hussein, in addition to being a brutal dictator, as an "environmental terrorist." However, the story was a lie, "a brilliant piece of propaganda"

(Knightley, 2000, p. 497). The oil slick that killed the cormorant was caused by Americans who had bombed an Iraqi tanker:

> It was to take nearly another month before an Associated Press story said a Saudi official had confirmed that the first crude oil to wash up on Saudi shores had resulted from an American attack and that Allied attacks were responsible for about a third of the oil pollution in Saudi waters. (Knightley, 2000, p. 498)

The second problem is that newsmakers report about events by framing them, and as a result, conflicts are cast within a specific definitional frame. For example, they may be termed insurgences, struggles of liberation, terrorism, or civil wars. These frames are often constructed by the primary definers of the news, such as politicians, who use skilled "perception managers" to sell their interpretation of reality. Furthermore, by and large, media tend to frame conflicts in terms of either/or choices.

Journalism is the art of telling stories, and this narrative format of news reporting implies the use of definitional frames. Through journalists, the parties in a conflict tell their stories, and their narratives change as the conflict develops. This often "entails a transformation from a narrative of victimization to one of evolution and empowerment" (Pruitt & Kim, 2004, p. 203). Pruitt and Kim went on to explain that

> Each side has its own narrative and, when conflict is severe, the two parties often interpret the same events in radically different ways. Thus, Israelis explain their military campaigns against Palestinians by talking about the Holocaust and the many times they have been attacked by the Arabs, who seem to be challenging their right to exist as a nation. Palestinians explain their assaults against Israel by talking about Israel's steady encroachment on their territory and freedoms. (2004, p. 202)

In the narrative of conflicts, metaphors play an essential role. Pruitt and Kim stated that "Some metaphors intensify a conflict and make it harder to solve" (2004, p. 202). They provided an example of the metaphors that the parties in the conflict in Northern Ireland used: The Irish Republican Army used "colonialism" to describe the role of the British army, and the British government used "criminality" to describe IRA activities. These were very negative metaphors that needed to be discarded for the peace process to move ahead.

Moreover, after the 9/11 attacks, governments and media routinely used the "war" metaphor. The attacks were called "acts of war," and the pursuit of the perpetrators was coined the "war on terror." Doing so focused attention on the military approach to the conflict and ignored the issues that caused the terrorists to act.

The third problem relates to a difficult question that media reporting about conflict raises: Should the horrendous and bloody pictures of warfare be publicized? Susan Sontag wrote about this in her book *Regarding the Pain of Others* (2002), arguing that these pictures tell us what people do to each other and that we should never forget this. Without the painful images of wounded and maimed children, audiences might be led to believe that wars can be "clean" and may forget that in modern warfare, air raids inevitably take numerous lives of young children.

This does raise the question: Does showing people's suffering make audiences realize the insanity and the disgrace of war, or would this rather motivate people to engage in more violence and revenge? It is not certain what the effects would be, but perhaps this is the wrong question altogether. We should probably ask: What would be the effect if we did not permanently and realistically show the horrors of warfare? If we did not demonstrate to each other what we are capable of, this obscuration would make it easier for those who initiate and want war to get away with it, contending that their wars are necessary and legitimate. The masquerade provides politicians and military ample space to distort the truth about their wars. However, shocking images and stories may not change the human propensity to lethal conflict. Yet, the fact that we have to confront human-made damage daily can be seen as a minimal morality. The least we can do is not to forget the victims. When Elie Wiesel received the Nobel Peace Prize in 1986, he said, "What all these victims need above all is to know that they are not alone, that we are not forgetting them, that when their voices are stifled, we shall lend them ours, that while their freedom depends on ours, the quality of our freedom depends on theirs" (Weisel, 1986).

In this same spirit, it should be noted that the Obama government reversed in 2009 an earlier decision by the Bush administration, lifting the ban on media coverage of the flag-draped coffins of war victims arriving home in the United States.

Finally, the fourth problem is media's tendency to suggest that killing is easy. Dave Grossman (1995, p. 35) observed that "The media in our modern information society have done much to perpetuate the myth of easy killing and have thereby become part of society's unspoken conspiracy of deception that glorifies killing and war." As an example, James Bond and his entertainment colleagues suggest that killing is easy. Contrary to what media contents suggest, humans have strong inhibitions against killing members of their own species. Grossman went on to state that "The media's depiction of violence tries to tell us that men can easily throw off the moral inhibitions of a lifetime—and whatever other instinctive restraint exists—and kill casually and guiltlessly in combat. Men who have killed and talk about it, tell a different tale" (p. 88).

STUDIES ON MEDIA VIOLENCE

In the media and communication research literature, one finds numerous studies on the relationship between media and violent behavior. Do such studies help us understand the role of media in the escalation spiral?

Although media and politicians have often been very certain about the media-violence equation, most academic studies tend to use prudent and provisional language when they find an association between media violence and aggressive human behavior. Common expressions are that media "may" promote violence in some children, that studies provide support for the "conjecture" that TV violence leads to violent behavior, or that watching TV violence "appears" to be related to actual violent conduct. One hardly finds strong convincing empirical evidence. The quality of data collection is rarely if ever questioned. This is a serious problem because the reliability and validity of much empirical material is very doubtful, such as when data are collected under highly unnatural laboratory conditions. Additionally, methodological flaws, such as taking correlations for causal connections, are not discussed in many studies.

These critiques do not deny that media could have an effect on people's behavior. However, even when effects are plausible, they are not yet convincingly scientifically demonstrated. Long-term effects of media on violence in society are still mainly a matter of conjecture and uncertainty.

Surveying the existing literature,[1] the conclusion that Schramm, Lyle, and Parker reached in 1961 still seems valid:

> For some children, under some conditions, some television is harmful. For other children, under most conditions, or for the same children under other conditions, it may be beneficial. For most children, under

most conditions, most television is probably neither particularly harmful nor particularly beneficial. (p. 1)

This prudent observation is likely to go beyond TV and also apply to new media such as the Internet and computer games.

Moreover, even if the findings did offer hard evidence, they could not simply be applied to collective behavior. The key problem for the present study is that the studies reviewed here all pertain to individual and interpersonal aggression, which teaches us little about collective aggression and intergroup aggression. In fact, we know very little about media and interpersonal destructive aggression, and we know even less about media and collective destructive aggression.

The core problem we face when exploring the relations between media performance and human behavior is people's obsession with causality. The obsessive drive to find causal connections is so strong that scientists often forget that correlations do not necessarily prove causal connections. That A and B occur together does not prove that A causes B or vice versa. Nonetheless, discovery causality is very attractive. It brings academics political popularity, better fundraising chances, and media attention. Media are most interested in science when causal connections are announced—between media violence and aggressive behavior, between smoking and cancer, between flying and environmental destruction, or between food and health. Causality assumes a simple world of one-to-one linear relations, but more often than not, scientists can only demonstrate (with grave reservations) a correlation and then speculate, hypothesize, and guess. The "causality obsession" is fatal for gaining a realistic understanding of the world in which we live. We exist in a reality of multiple causalities, and it is probably impossible to single out one specific causal factor ever.

Consequently, the present study does not seek the confirmation of a causality hypothesis on media performance and collective aggressive behavior. As mentioned in the introduction, this search is of a heuristic nature: I am trying to discover what questions we need to ask. This means looking at "facilitation" and asking whether media play a role in creating space for collective destructive aggression. The leading question is not whether media cause this, but rather whether they are among the factors that facilitate killing and humiliating fellow human beings.

The question about the facilitating role of media obviously raises the perennial issue of media power: Do media have power? That they do is often claimed and subsequently condemned by politicians. However, in the strict sense of power as the coercive capacity to make people do things they would otherwise not do, media have no power. They have no sanctions, punishments, physical threats, or violent means at their disposal. Nevertheless, media do have influence. They are capable of exposing, publicizing, and accusing. For instance, a 1995 documentary about Chinese orphanages, *The Dying Rooms* by Kate Blewett, created a global outcry of indignation and had a great deal of influence worldwide. Thus, when the general public has knowledge, awareness, and rage about what happens, people may put considerable pressures on a given government, which may lead to new policies and substantial changes. In this instance, the media did not, however, possess the coercive power to force the Chinese government to do anything it would not want to do. The same can be said about the much-acclaimed and -criticized documentaries of filmmaker Michael Moore. They may have great public influence, opening people's eyes and raising awareness, but his critical accounts of the banking industry, for example, do not have the power to arrest and jail bankers.

This, then, narrows the leading question to how the influence that media may have facilitates collective evil.

MEDIA AND ANXIETY

"Developments in the past two decades suggest, indeed, that fear stimulation has become an overwhelming temptation for media in a variety of sectors from commercial pitchmen to the fine arts."

Peter N. Stearns (2006)

Most human anxiety is related to perceived dangers of future conditions, and such perceptions are socially mediated. In social mediation processes, media—both entertainment and news media as well as both conventional and new media—have become central institutions. Day after day, they offer a discourse of anxiety. Every single day, the media warn us of some impending danger.

Thus, they amplify our already existing existential anxiety, and doing so create a perspective on the world and on people's place within this world. Whether or not this perspective leads to the perpetration of evil deeds depends on a variety of both external and internal variables.

Around the world one finds in many radio and television newscasts and newspapers' lead articles strong references to crises—food crisis, oil crisis, climate crisis, population crisis, terrorism crisis—as well as fear and risk.

Much of this language has little to do with actual world incidents. Although over a longer time span—1986–2007—terrorist incidents have declined, governments and their complicit media maintain a credible global threat.

There is a growing cottage industry of "anxiety marketers," offering their services to help with concerns people might not even have realized they harbored. These concerns are about health, lifestyles, afterlife styles (funeral fashion), appearance, aging, financial status, home security, kids with ADHD, marital stress, sexual performance, the size and appearance of their genitalia, culinary expertise, vinological knowledge, the psychopathology of their pets, or garden architecture (even if they have no garden). In this industry, the news and entertainment media are key vehicles for promoting anxiety and contributors to an anxious perspective on the world. Most of the popular perceptions on the dangers of crime and terrorism are mediated to people by news reports and entertainment programs.

People become anxious when media tell them there is something wrong with them (like advertising or medical TV programs do), when they suggest uncertain and probably very troubled futures (like in daily newscasts about issues such as the credit crisis), or by making them fearful (with discourses on terror, evil, and war).

Media render anxiety a shared perspective on life. For the first time in history, millions of people across the globe can watch simultaneously stories of fear and crisis. For these global audiences, the media construct a world that is filled with warnings that the world is a dangerous place and that things may get worse.

According to Furedi's observation (1997), the media amplify people's sense of risk and danger but do not cause it. They amplify people's disposition to expect that things will work out the wrong way by constantly warning of one or another danger. As David Altheide observed,

> Fear has become a staple of popular culture, ranging from fun to dread. Americans trade on fear. News agencies report it, produce entertainment messages (other than news) about it, and promote it, police and other agencies of social control market it. And audiences watch it, read it, and, according to numerous mass entertainment spokespersons, demand it. (2002, p. 64)

Altheide's research also led him to conclude that "Fear is more prevalent in news today than it was several years ago, and it appears in more sections of the newspaper. This is particularly true of headlines" (p. 99).

Fear is a major feature of the entertainment format of popular culture. Altheide went on to observe that

In an era in which information is packaged and manufactured, when popular culture is driven by entertainment formats, and when agents work to transform risks into fear with state-sponsored solutions, the social and the cultural become one. Fear is constructed and it is real. The entertainment-inspired frame is embodied in the emotions and justice of everyday life. (p. 196)

As Stefanie Grupp (2003) argued—on the basis of much empirical material—there has been a general shift from a fearsome life toward life with fearsome media. It can indeed be argued that daily life in European medieval times was in permanent, direct danger and that daily fears in modern times are largely mediated through news and entertainment.

Among the emotions that constitute anxiety, fear has become a particularly dominant feature of media discourse. Certainly after the 9/11 events the U.S. media prominently displayed a discourse of fear. Since then, many media have generously and uncritically adopted the threat rhetoric by injudiciously using words like war, rogue states, and axis of evil, or by describing enemies with animal metaphors.

The media's amplification of anxiety can be observed in connection with climate change, global finance, and psychiatric drugs.

Climate Crisis

In 1986 the German magazine *Der Spiegel* constructed the notion of a climate disaster in a cover story. The cover showed the Cathedral in Cologne with its steeple barely rising above the water of the North Sea. More recently—2006—the documentary *An Inconvenient Truth*, produced by former U.S. Vice President and Nobel Prize winner Al Gore, became a major vehicle in the global spread of climate anxiety, as did the 2004 film *The Day After Tomorrow* (directed by Roland Emmerich and raking in over US$540 million). It can hardly be doubted that many people around the world have become anxious about global warming, dying polar bears, or global tsunamis. From international public opinion polls, we know that there is climate anxiety.

An important factor in creating this anxiety has undoubtedly been the powerful suggestion that there is global scientific consensus on climate change and the media's subsequent proliferation of this consensus. According to Al Gore, the UN Intergovernmental Panel on Climate Change (IPCC), and most of the international media, "the science is settled" (Solomon, 2008, p. 1). Consensus, however, is highly unlikely because science consists of a continuous process of "conjectures and refutations," as the title of the famous book by Karl Popper (1963) suggests. People should greet any announcements of a scientific consensus with a great deal of suspicion. In fact, in the climate change debate, one finds top scientists who disagree on various dimensions of the issue. The IPCC has always claimed that its position on climate change is supported by some 4,000 scientists, but it is likely that less than 100 climate researchers have been actively involved in IPCC reports and thousands of scientists have distanced themselves (such as the Oregon Petition Project) from the key IPCC hypothesis on the harmful effects of human use of hydrocarbons. Moreover, even if there would be consensus, it is still possible that the consensus is wrong!

The language of climate catastrophe is common in the media. There are more assumptions than facts in the public debate, and these are not as rigorously tested as scientific hypotheses would require. In the global debate, there is little room allowed for uncertainty and critical questions about the manipulation of data; the use of inadequate statistical models or of models that are too broad to take into account such small factors as the role of clouds; the lack of longitudinal perspectives; the type of linear reasoning that is characteristic of Western thought; a tunnel vision that identifies only one suspect (human-produced CO_2) and that searches no further for other possible suspects; and, lastly, the pretense of forecasting when we can hardly predict tomorrow's weather.

Amidst all the alarmism and environmental fundamentalism, there is remarkably little critical investigation into the role and mandate of the IPCC. Could it be that the IPCC is primarily a governmental mechanism to prove that disaster is imminent and that human-made CO_2 is to blame? Could it be that the panel does not point to inadequate, corrupt, or nonexistent state policies on poverty reduction, health and hygiene, energy sources, and water management as causes of such disasters as the return of malaria in Third World cities? What does it mean that the panel has changed positions over its past four reports on issues like the rise of sea levels? What does it mean that the Fourth Assessment Report of the IPCC (2007) presents erroneous information about the melting of Himalaya glaciers?

What does it mean that the IPCC deliberately causes widespread anxiety? Its vice president, John Houghton, said in 1994 that if we do not announce catastrophes, nobody will listen, and IPCC president Rajendra Pachauri stated, "I hope this will shock people and governments into taking action" (Bachmann, 2008, p. 9). The risk this implies is that the global climate opinion makers follow the advice of climatologist Stephan

Schneider, who finds that one should use anything that raises awareness without raising doubts about climate change, preferably dramatic
statements (Furedi, 2005).

The media do not cause climate anxiety. They side either with the
alarmists or with the skeptics, amplifying the narratives and the policy
recommendations of the side they choose. By and large, they fail to
point to a factor that unites the different parties—uncertainty. It is
reasonable to guess that societal emotional strain is related to the certainty with which different inflated egos in the climate debate give their
audiences mutually exclusive advice. Although all parties in the global
climate debate are haunted by the same fundamental uncertainty, they
nonetheless obscure this with eloquent hunches and assumptions that
are presented as facts.

However, I should add that climate change is obviously an urgent
problem that needs world attention. It would be foolish to act as if
nothing is wrong with global climatic conditions and ignore the serious effects this has on people worldwide. Yet deliberately creating
societal anxiety and refusing to acknowledge uncertainty are only likely
to compound the problems; obstruct long-term, sustainable solutions;
and contribute to escalating societal conflict.

Mental Health Crisis

A similar analysis can be conducted on global media advertising for
pharmaceutical products, especially psychopharmaca. These are drugs
drug companies brought on the market, suggesting they help cope with
mental diseases. Again, as with climate change, it would be irrespon-
sible to ignore the seriousness of mental disorders and their effects on
individuals and societies. It would also be rather shortsighted not to
acknowledge the possibility of biological causes of psychological problems
and to refuse scientific exploration of biochemical treatment.

This being said, we turn to the core issue. We have to admit that—
scientifically speaking—there is no reliable biochemical evidence for
the diagnosis of mental disorders and little—if any—knowledge about
effective treatment. The psychiatric discipline tends to label certain human conditions mental disorders not because of scientific research but
through majority votes in meetings of the American Psychiatric Association. Situations that are a normal part of human life (e.g., people
experiencing their daily functioning as unsatisfactory, disturbing, or as
inimical to their expectations and hopes about life) become—in the

psychiatric view—diseases. Over the past fifty years, the discipline has added generously to the numbers of personality disorders that it lists in the standard work for disorder, the Diagnostic and Statistical Manual of Mental Disorders. Its first issue in 1952 proposed 112 disorders, and by 1994 the number had risen to 374 entries.

One problem with labeling human conditions as psychiatric diseases is that the diagnosis—unlike in the case of physical disorders—does not use the evidence of blood and urine tests, X-rays, or blood pressure measurements. The diagnosis is an opinion often arrived at in very limited time and often not even by a psychiatric expert but instead by a general practitioner. For the treatment of physical disorders, doctors often prescribe chemical products.[2] Increasingly, however, the same happens with the treatment of mental disorders. In the United States alone, the market for psychiatric drugs reached US$40.3 billion in 2008. In fact, one antipsychosis drug, Seroquel, was prescribed in 2009 to some 26 million people worldwide (Pringle, 2009, December 12). In order to reach such sales levels, it is necessary to make people anxious about their mental condition and to present normal experiences of stress, anger, or grief as a mental disorder that needs a chemical cure.

Through extensive advertising, medical articles in the popular press, and talk shows, the psychiatric industry has managed to make large numbers of people sufficiently emotionally strained to take addictive and often toxic pills. All this marketing and psychiatric propaganda has—among other things—very effectively sold the idea to parents that they should be fearful of normal childish behavior and should see behavioral problems as diseases that should be treated with drugs that are stronger than cocaine. Kids who run around a lot, argue with their parents, lose their temper, or have problems learning can be labeled mentally deficient and put on life-long medication.

Anxiety in the sense of emotional strain is a condition that makes people vulnerable to manipulation. It is not a mental disorder—as psychopharmacological advertising suggests—that needs medication. Prescribing anti-anxiety drugs to anxious societies may be a dream of the psychiatric and pharmaceutical industries, but it is consolidating the road toward drugged societies. Anxiety needs to be recognized, kept within controllable proportions, and dealt with through nonaddictive measures. However, the drug culture suppresses human faculties of independent reasoning and reflexive criticism. It neutralizes people's real-life context, leads them away from productive and creative lifestyles, and renders them more vulnerable to conflict escalation.

Financial Crisis

Another anxiety-related topic in international media concerns developments in the world of finance and banking. In international media, the
words most often used in reporting about the financial problems in the
banking world were "fear" and "crisis." Although the media certainly
did not cause the credit troubles, by constantly reporting in terms of
impending global disaster, they may have amplified societal feelings of
anxiety and, thus, contributed to a loss of societal confidence in financial institutions. Certainly, robbers should be exposed as robbers and
not hailed as innocent people, but media logic tends toward unwar-
ranted generalizations with captions such as "investors fear recession":
Does this mean all investors? Can the news source claim to have asked
all or at least a majority of investors? Generalizing judgments such as
this undermined the whole system without sufficient analysis of what
societies could do about stopping the robbery. Media do not make
notations on stock exchanges, but an avalanche of negative news about
a company may further reinforce a downward trend. Journalists should
obviously expose the bad guys, but media logic often glosses over the
possibility that not all the guys are bad and that media labeling does
require substantial argument and documentation. Journalists—though
there are exceptions—often lack the expertise and the political savvy
to recognize that they (too often) are taken by surprise. Dutch media
expert Jan Kleinnijenhuis, commenting on his research on the role
of newspapers during the "credit crisis," wondered why most Dutch
newspapers were very positive about the Dutch government action to
"nationalize" the bank Fortis on October 3, 2008, and yet did not
foresee the need for this and recommend it earlier (Kleinnijenhuis,
2008, p. 15). The credit issue was mainly described as an uncontrollable phenomenon, which led Kleinnijenhuis to suggest that if journalists would explain how the financial system operates, fear and panic
could be prevented.

MEDIA AND AGITATION

Agitation identifies the scapegoat of "our" suffering and approves of
violence against "them." Worldwide, media provide political leaders
with a broad platform for their agitation in the form of inflammatory,
exclusionary, and divisionary rhetoric. Around the world, media are
complicit in political leaders' inciting the public to collective violence.

Often—and uncritically—media give a podium to some of the world's most dangerous agitators. From the Nazi publication *Der Stürmer* to the Rwandan Radio Television *Libre de Mille Collines*, there are many examples of media complicity in political incitement to genocidal or politicidal killings. Angry political leaders need a public platform, and mass media often provide this without asking too many questions.

For example, governments have often much too easily enlisted media in their war efforts. Leaders may present a convincing narrative on terrorism, for example, but "political discourses only rise to prominence ... when other social actors—the media in particular—amplify the language across the wider society" (Jackson, 2005, p. 154). Again, the major role of the media is to amplify the official political discourse. As Richard Jackson proposed (2005, p. 154), "This is exactly what happened in the years following September 11, 2001: the media, together with other important actors, reproduced the official discourse in a relatively unmediated fashion, while at the same time silencing and marginalising alternative narratives." Key components of the 9/11 Bush presidential agitation were references to the "axis of evil," "acts of mass murder," "barbaric regimes," "a new war," "evil empire," "threats to our way of life," and the "fight to save the civilized world." Others in the Bush administration followed suit, framing the 9/11 attacks in the discourse of good versus evil: "a strike against those values that separate us from animals" (James Baker, 2001, September 23), or "to fight this evil wherever it exists ... to ensure the line between the civil and the savage" (John Ashcroft, 2001, September 24).

In his "Address to the Nation" on September 11, 2001, George W. Bush proclaimed, "Today our nation saw evil, the very worst of human nature." Furthermore, in 2002 in a speech at West Point Military Academy, the president said, "We are in a conflict between good and evil, and America will call evil by its name." This political discourse transformed worldwide into the media discourse. What's more, it helped people to identify the culprits and legitimized strong action against them.

A favorite word in the agitational discourse was "evil." In post–9/11 rhetoric, "evil" became self-understood, obvious, not in need of further inquiry. As Richard J. Bernstein commented,

> "Evil" tends to be used in an excessively vague and permissive manner in order to condemn whatever one finds abhorrent.... [It] is used in a highly selective and self-serving manner.... There have been an increasing number of reliable reports about the widespread use of torture and

deliberate humiliation not only at Abu Ghraib, but also throughout Iraq. And the Red Cross has reported that practices "tantamount to torture" have taken place at prison in Guantanamo Bay.... I do not know of a single statement by a member of the current United States administration who has condemned these practices as *evil.* (2005, p. 97)

Media's amplification of the rhetoric of evil served the purpose of linking "evil" with "them" and equating "us" with those who do not commit evil deeds. Bernstein went on to state that

After all, we are the good guys who are dedicated to spreading democracy and freedom, and we are fighting the bad guys—the evil ones. In a world where there is a stark black-and-white opposition between good and evil, good guys do not commit evil atrocities. (2005, p. 98)

This general tendency to reproduce leadership discourse is part of the troubled relationship between media and leaders. By and large, media give ample space and prominence to those in political leadership. This is strikingly manifest in the so-called photo opportunities with the world's leaders. They gather behind closed doors to decide ordinary peoples' fates, and in great generosity they concede to a group photo that presents them as if they were God's chosen angels. The media portrayal of political leaders in images such as these suggests competence, trustworthiness, rationality, and sanity.

Powerful elites tend to enjoy enormous prestige. Media representations of leaders create "celebrity" status for political leaders, thus transforming them into respected celebrities. According to P. Eric Louw (2005, p. 172), "Celebrities appear important because the media make them important. They are in the media because the public is interested in them, but the public is interested because the media generate that interest." Celebrities are manufactured, and then media blur the lines between politicians and other celebrities:

For spin-doctors, manufacturing a popular celebrity politician represents the ultimate success.... Ironically, all those involved in manufacturing celebrity politicians have a vested interest in denying celebrity-ness is an organized construction—journalists deny complicity because that would be an admission that spin-doctors can manipulate them ... PRs deny complicity because of negativity towards their "dark arts" ... and politicians deny they are "constructed" because that would undermine their "leadership" image. (Louw, 2005, p. 175)

Furthermore, the celebrity politician is presented as both like us and not like us. He is the combination of being in command and being in touch with ordinary folks (Louw, 2005, p. 176).

The political spectacle, therefore, is an arena of delusions. However, media hide these chimera from the public eye by creating a symbolic universe that suggests responsibility and genuine concern. Particularly through press photos, the media widely disseminate the key symbolic representations of political leadership.

This imagery presents the political "capo" as a "Roi Soleil" through images that evoke those of monarchs greeting and waving at their subjects. The media also portray the leader as hero through images of victory, as a concerned benefactor, as a pop star, or as an ordinary Joe Six-Pack. Through such essential symbolic representations, the political spectacle obscures the fact that political leaders more often than not are autists, narcissists, or megalomaniacs who stand on the political stage as if they were caring, altruistic, and ordinary human beings. It is true that the powerful are different from the ordinary people they govern, but the most significant lie they disseminate is that they are *not* powerful. Media representations tend to obscure that there are seriously disturbing elements in the exercise of power.

Those who are involved in it require certain personality characteristics that, in the context of daily life, are very disturbing. As Charles Wright Mills wrote,

> few individuals in positions of such authority can long resist the temptation to base their self-images, at least in part, upon the sounding board of the collectivity which they head.... When he speaks in the name of the country or its cause, its past glory also echoes in his ears. (1956, p. 357)

Only rarely do the governed know how sick and weak those who govern them really are. Many important leaders of the nineteenth and twentieth century were manic depressive, such as Abraham Lincoln, Theodore Roosevelt, Winston Churchill, Nikita Chroesjtsjov, and Lyndon Johnson (D. Owen, 2008). Furthermore, the world leaders who met at Yalta in 1945 to decide the future of Europe were Churchill, an alcoholic with serious heart failure; Roosevelt, who suffered heart problems; and Stalin, a paranoid mass murderer.

Power is intoxicating, and many prominent leaders, such as Adolf Hitler, Joseph Stalin, Mao Zedong, Pol Pot, and Idi Amin, were guided by megalomaniac perceptions of their own power and significance. The megalomanic personality is absolutely convinced of his or her own beliefs and is increasingly incapable of accepting critical comments and objections, is blind to his own failure, and follows one-dimensional and (often wrong) biased interpretations of the reality in which (the often wrong) decisions will be made.

Many U.S. presidents suffered from serious mental disorders, such as depression (Thomas Woodrow Wilson), pyschosis/paranoia (Richard Nixon), bipolarity (Lyndon Johnson), or narcissism (George W. Bush). What's more, political leaders—among them Theodore Roosevelt, John F. Kennedy, and François Mitterrand—have also lied about their health. As David Owen informed us, U.S. president Kennedy took drugs that today would disqualify him from participating in the Tour de France.

Consequently, political leaders often have unrealistic images of their own power. This pathology of power manifests itself, among other ways, in an exaggerated self-perception of power. Boulding (1990, p. 66) illustrated this when he discussed Hitler, who "started a war that led to his own suicide, the total destruction of all his ideas, immense destruction of Germany, and the establishment of Israel."

As a final point, leaders obviously make news, and it would be unrealistic to ignore them. However, news media could do more to expose those in leadership who, for reasons of physical or mental deficiencies, have difficulty balancing reason and emotion and who have a penchant for engaging in agitating behavior. The minimum that media could do is to be more economic with photo sessions. What a great day it would be for democracy and sanity if the news photographers stayed home for once and left the world's leaders without a platform!

MEDIA AND ALIENATION

> "Many of the conflicts and barbarities in the world are sustained through the illusion of a unique and choiceless identity."
>
> Amartya Sen (2006)

The core of alienation is the creation of fundamental rifts between adversaries. Media contribute to this through the amplification of vilifying and demonizing language. One illustration is the metaphor of the "rogue state" that has been widely used by the media to refer to other nations. This is a powerful construct in strengthening the distance between "our" civilization and "their" savagery. The "rogue" nations are actors outside the world community. They are different from "civilized" nations, so violence against them is legitimate. By using dehumanizing language against enemies, the media encourages violence, as Ayotte and Moore (2008, p. 85) wrote: "If terrorists are described as less than human, in addition to being 'evil', not only there is no reason to reflect upon one's own character and behavior, but also there is less reason to question violence as a default counter-terrorism strategy." They went on to provide examples of such dehumanization, citing an article in *Newsweek* on October 1, 2002, in which the writer used this kind of language to dehumanize the enemy: "for every terror cell beheaded two more will crawl out of the swamps ... that swamps can never be drained in land that drips with the blood of martyrs" (p. 86). Demonizing the enemy makes it easy and helps justify killing them, thus making it unnecessary to question the enemy's motives, grievances, or demands.

Furthermore, Ayotte and Moore went on to note that "dehumanizing language often represents the 'ultimate weapon' in war, because it creates mental frameworks within which moral norms are relaxed" (2008, p. 86). Thus, when the media uses dehumanizing discourse, it constructs the opposition between us and the savages, and when the savages belong to non-Western countries, the opposition becomes easily racially colored. As Cloud argued, "This racism, thinly veiled as a cultural and not a racial logic, becomes most visible as racism when it refers metaphorically to Arabs and Muslims as animals" (2008, p. 229). Examples of this kind of rhetoric include popular descriptions of terrorists as sharks or breeds of savages.

Dehumanizing Language and Genocide

In most internal violent conflicts, local media are used to reinforce sectarian categorizations; support feelings of ethnic, racial, or religious superiority; and legitimize destructive action. In Rwanda, despite tribal animosity, for decades Hutu and Tutsi lived together and intermarried, attended the same schools, drank at the same bars, and so forth. By 1990, however, the Hutu-dominated newspapers and radio were calling for an extermination of the minority Tutsi (Power, 2002, pp. 337–340). The media depicted the Tutsi as arrogant, privileged immigrants who were "enemies of the people."

Then, in 1994, over the course of just a few months, somewhere between 500,000 and 1 million Tutsis were killed by Hutus. According to Kellow and Steeves,

Although several Rwandan media have been accused of inciting the genocide that began in April, by far the most influential was Radio-Télévision Libre des Mille Collines (RTLM). Many survivors believe that the extent of the killing and later exodus would not have happened without RTLM. It became the government voice in demanding genocide. (1998, p. 117)

The station managed to attract a large audience (military, peasants, young people) and recruited very persuasive journalists and announcers, who "encouraged Hutu hatred and slaughter of the Tutsis by talking about the Tutsi hate of the Hutus. The frequent use of popular culture, biblical references and familiar historical context strengthened the power of the broadcasts" (Kellow & Steeves, 1998, p. 119). In fact, RTLM broadcast "orders to exterminate all Tutsis," and the transcript from one broadcast read, "Finish them off … exterminate them … sweep them out of the country" (Kellow & Steeves, 1998, p. 120). The RTLM repeatedly broadcast messages in which Tutsis were slandered, ridiculed, and depicted as despicable. Then, on 4 June, 1994, RTLM journalist Kantano Habimana told listeners that

They should all stand up so that we kill the Inkotanyi and exterminate them … the reason we will exterminate them is that they belong to one ethnic group. Look at the person's height and his physical appearance. Just look at his small nose and then break it. (from the transcript of the proceedings of the International Rwanda Tribunal)

The RTLM informed Hutu militia where Tutsis—who were referred to as "cockroaches"—were hiding so they could be murdered. Thus, the media made Hutus believe that the Tutsis deserved to be eliminated, and this rhetorical manipulation resulted in a horrifying bloodbath. The propaganda was so effective that people killed their own neighbors, who had been living in peace beside them for many years. Ordinary people turned into crazed killing machines because media made them believe that the Tutsis were a dangerous and hideous enemy that lived next door.

Incitement to destruction also took place in media in Burundi during the 1990s, following a pattern similar to the lead-up to the Rwandan genocide, in which the media framed local conflict in ethnic terms and called for groups to destroy each other. In the former Yugoslavia, much the same happened, as Predrag Simic wrote in 1994,

The function of war propaganda disseminated by the conflicting parties has been, by turn, to mobilize and intimidate, glorify and demonize, and justify and accuse, bearing out the assumption that the media bears a large part of the responsibility for the outbreak and tragic course of the war in former Yugoslavia. (Kellow & Steeves, 1998, p. 126)

Furthermore, in the Balkan conflict, the media played a crucial role. Serbs, Croats, and Bosnians all used television in particular for their propagandistic purposes. Serbian TV journalists who refused to participate were fired or even killed. The daily TV news—watched by some 60% of the population—was strongly nationalist and ethnically prejudiced. The programs exaggerated enormously the threat from Bosnian Muslims and Croats, presenting the war as both inevitable and justified. Similar reporting occurred in Croatia, and the government in Bosnia-Herzegovina also used this propagandistic approach. The media reported lost battles as victories and ignored or downplayed war crimes by "our" side.

In 2002, in Côte d'Ivoire, most media were disseminating the kind of propaganda among political parties and religious and ethnic groups that was prevalent in Rwanda preceding the genocide, and this kind of media incitement contributed greatly to a civil war, which lasted from 2002 to 2007.

Additionally, during the 2007 Kenyan elections, local ("vernacular") radio stations incited fear and hate. These stations were routinely partisan and their talk shows in particular provided opportunities for hate speech (BBC, 2008, p. 2). Although a comparison with 1994 Rwanda does not seem fair, one commentator observed that "We did not reach the Radio Milles Collines level, but we were not very far from it ... some presenters were clearly happy that a caller was saying certain things" (BBC, 2008, p. 5). Usually these "certain things" involved calling on people to stand up and fight. There is no evidence that connects local media to the organization of violence, but in explosive situations, where people are divided along ethnic lines, we should expect media to operate prudently with the language they use. Accordingly, the Kenyan mainstream media have tried to cover events in ways that were intended to calm down the emotions, using careful language and avoiding references to tribal affiliations. By and large, however, the community of journalists and editors felt that the Kenyan media collectively failed in playing an independent and professional role in the national conflict. The BBC report goes on to state that "As politics has become more factionalised along political and ethnic grounds, the media—including much of the mainstream media—have been drawn into, and often aligned with different political interests" (2008, p. 9).

Hate speech in Kenya was also disseminated through such new media technologies as mobile telephones and weblogs (which also happened at an extensive scale in Kashmir, India). Contending ethnic groups have used SMS messaging to incite ethnic hatred and violence, and although the blogosphere offered democratic debate, it also presented virulent hate campaigns. These media, which play a crucial role spreading rumors, are difficult if not impossible to regulate, even though monitoring and filtering SMS and blog traffic is technically possible. Some governments have banned SMS texts during elections, like the Ethiopian government did in 2005, but if people cannot SMS, they switch to weblogs, and if that is impossible, then they switch back to SMS. As always, the problem is too serious to expect that prohibiting the use of certain message carriers can solve it.

The Huntington Thesis

In a 1993 article in *Foreign Affairs*—and the precursor of his well-known book *The Clash of Civilizations and the Remaking of World Order* (1997)—Huntington wrote,

> It is my hypothesis that the fundamental source of conflict in this new world will not primarily be ideological or primarily economic. The great divisions among human kind and the dominating source of conflict will be cultural.... The clash of civilizations will dominate global politics. The fault line between civilizations will be the battle lines of the future. (1993, p. 22)

The main argument of his thesis is that future world conflict will play out along cultural and religious differences. Huntington sees recent wars in Bosnia, Kashmir, and Chechnya as conflicts between civilizations.

The empirical historical data render this thesis very doubtful because civilizations are never closed, singular, and monolithic entities, and, furthermore, in the past, most conflicts were not civilizational. However, worldwide, media gave Huntington's book *The Clash of Civilizations* a global podium, transforming it into a convenient construction that helped numerous people believe that the world can be divided into "our" and "their" civilizations and that these two civilizations are at war. Although the thesis was never taken very seriously by scholars in matters of international and intercultural relations, after 9/11, media incorporated it into their news discourse. Illustrations can be found in influential media such as the *New York Times, Wall Street Journal, Washington Post, Newsweek,* and the major U.S. TV networks (Abrahamian, 2003, p. 530). For many influential media around the world, the thesis became the key guide to reporting and interpreting the 9/11 events. As cited in Abrahamian (2003): the *New York Times* wrote that the hijackers wanted to "bring about a new order of purity and Islamic righteousness"; the *Wall Street Journal* reported that "a barbaric culture had declared war" (September 20, 2001); editor Richard Lowry of the *National Review* (on National Public Radio, December 15, 2001) informed the audience that Muslims live in a completely "alien culture"; and Fuad Ajami, in *U.S. News and World Report* (November 26, 2001) called Al Jazeera a "Muslim television station" and pleaded for its removal. Well-known intellectuals like Salman Rushdie, Robert Kaplan, Ian Buruma, and Bernard Lewis—with qualifications and other words—accepted the Huntington thesis, and their positions received prominent media exposure. In fact, media star Bernard Lewis, the Middle East specialist, gave numerous TV interviews on the "roots of Muslim rage" (*Atlantic Monthly,* September 1990) and was applauded by Paul Wolfowitz as a "great Anglo-American scholar" (Abrahamian, 2003, p. 541). It seems plausible to think that the backlash against Arabs in the United States (like the imprisonment without charges of some 1,200 Muslims) was related to the media's amplification of the culturalist discourse. Fox TV news also gave Reverend Pat Roberts a broad public platform to proclaim that "Muslims were worse than Nazis" (reported by the *Washington Post,* December 2, 2002).

Furthermore, Norwegian and Danish newspapers also used the Huntington thesis frequently in connection with the commotion around the Mohammed cartoons, thus framing the conflict between free speech and religious insult as a clash of civilizations.

The danger of Huntington's *Clash of Civilizations* is that it assumes that people's identities are based on civilizations and that people can be brought under civilizational categorizations. The assumption implies the dangerous notion of choiceless singularity (Sen, 2006). Moreover, the thesis very much represents us-versus-them thinking, in which the dangerous "them" are primarily Muslims. Ours is the "Age of Muslim Wars," as Huntington suggested in *Newsweek* (January 3, 2002).

Killing the enemy becomes easier when people think of themselves as part of a singular identity and of others a part of another singular identity. As Amartya Sen (2006) observed regarding the Hindu-Muslim riots in the 1940s,

> The political instigators who urged the killing ... managed to persuade many otherwise peaceable people of both communities to turn into dedicated thugs. They were made to think of themselves only as Hindus or only as Muslims ... and as absolutely nothing else: not Indians, not subcontinentals, not Asians, not members of a shared human race. (p. 172)

To paraphrase Sen, a major source of alienation in the contemporary world is the presumption that people can be uniquely categorized based on religion or culture. Huntington proposed an essentialist, culturalist discourse about the others. This means that cultural characteristics—in the narrow sense of ethnic differences—are seen as essential and unchangeable rather than contextual and, thus, open to change.[3]

MEDIA AND ACCUSATION IN A MIRROR

When looking at the media that prepare people for genocidal action, one often finds the stories about how the "others" threaten us. In his closing arguments against Jean-Paul Akayesu (on March 19, 1998), Pierre Prosper, the prosecutor for the International Criminal Tribunal for Rwanda, explained the Hutu propaganda techniques. He described how media accused the Tutsi of planning a genocide, which was, in fact, planned against them. He called this "accusation in a mirror." In the Rwandan newspaper *Kangura*, people would read that the Inyenzi (Tutsis) have grudges against the Hutu, and to preserve "us," the Hutu needed to destroy "them." Thus, the Hutu were faced with what they saw as an unprecedented threat and had to act in self-defense.

Examples of accusation in a mirror can be found on most pages of *Kangura*. Hutu people had "to protect themselves against the genocide so carefully orchestrated by the Hamites [Tutsi] thirsty for blood and for barbarian conquests...." Accusation in a mirror implies that bloody actions against opponents are recognized, but the responsibility for those activities is assigned to the victim.

In another example, in the anti-Semitic Nazi magazine *Der Stürmer* (first published on April 20, 1923), people could read "Die Juden Sind Unser Unglück" (Jews are our bad luck), and that Jews were "a parasite, an enemy, an evil-doer, a disseminator of diseases who must be destroyed in the interests of mankind." Most importantly, however, the magazine accused Jewry of being a danger to the German people, claiming that Jews endanger German lives and their extermination is the only solution to protect Germans. Editor of *Der Stürmer* Julius Streicher wrote that self-preservation requires crushing the head of the serpent.[4]

Furthermore, in the violent confrontations in Kenya in 2008, the mechanism of accusation in a mirror became the dominant political tactic. Media encouraged the different ethnic parties to believe that their opponents intended to exterminate them. The Kikuyus were convinced that the Kalenjins were preparing their slaughter even as the Kalenjins accused the Kikuyus of plotting their extermination. Here again, propaganda worked to accuse others of what people were planning on doing themselves.

CONCLUSION

If we want to explore whether mass destruction of human dignity could revisit modern democratic states, we need to analyze whether today's most influential media—in terms of providing people with information about the world in which they live and, thus, shaping their perceptions of the others with whom they share this world—contribute to creating the key drivers of the escalation spiral: anxiety, agitation, alienation, and accusation in a mirror. The cases that I selected from an overwhelming volume of available data suggest there is sufficient cause for concern. Mass media offer a daily discourse of societal anxiety, provide public platforms for the rhetoric of angry leaders, facilitate alienation by adopting divisive frames, and make possible the self-defense argument.

One lesson to take from this chapter is that in order to better understand patterns of collective violence, we need to investigate the relationship between the sociocultural environment within which anxiety is generated, agitation is exercised, and alienation and accusation are cultivated and patterns of collective violence. Doing so requires detailed exploration of how the phases of the escalation spiral are socially mediated and how to position the media in these mediation processes. Are mass media indeed key facilitation mechanisms in the spiral of escalation?

Such a question requires innovative approaches to media research. This would seem easy because there is a common aspiration in the sciences to be innovative. The ideal is that scientists search for and are open to innovative ideas. In reality, however, many scientists are somewhat "neophobic," and rather inclined toward "epistemic conservatism." They tend to prefer trusted methods of research and accepted theories and concepts. They favor looking for the confirmation of what they do know already. Because of this, new information is often interpreted in accordance with information already received.

Although scientists like to claim that they strive to falsify their initial assumptions, in practice, their preference is to verify what they have previously concluded. This epistemic conservatism is often manifest in modalities of publication and processes of peer review. Peer reviewers often judge work by lesser-known colleagues and by newcomers with a great deal of skepticism. As such, if an article is based on a new, unknown or uncommon method, editors prefer to reject it. Thus, the academic establishment is not prone to taking risks. Often, submissions for scientific publication that take a totally unexpected approach meet such strict demands that they will not be published. Moreover, if they do get published, reviewers are likely to protect themselves by inserting many (often unnecessary) remarks and footnotes. What's more, a negative review tends to be more highly considered than a positive review. Most of today's scientific conferences are organized conservatively. Papers are read to colleagues who rarely listen and then published in journals hardly anybody reads.

The first challenge for serious research is to liberate the discipline from epistemic conservatism, challenging it to live up to the traditional scientific ideal of contributing new ideas and new ways of understanding. The second challenge for media studies is to "remember the future" and to incorporate future studies in its teaching and research. If one attends the conferences of the World Future Society, where professionals from many disciplines meet to develop foresight, innovation, and strategy, one finds that media and communication scholars are in short supply, if they participate at all. Few of the curricula in communication studies deal seriously with future studies. However, most of what will happen to communication processes and institutions will occur definitively in the future. Today, the field of future studies is no longer the domain of totally nonplausible projections but rather is developing into an incredibly rich domain of serious methodological and theoretical thinking about the future. Media research could find inspiration from a conversation in *Through the Looking Glass* where Alice says, "I can't remember things before they happen," and the White Queen replies, "It's a poor sort of memory that only works backwards" (Carroll, 1988, p. 254).[5]

CHAPTER 3

TAMING THE SPIRAL OF ESCALATION

↜

If indeed mass media facilitate escalating evil, we must question what role they can play in the taming of evil. Can they also facilitate the de-escalation of conflict?

COMMUNICATION AND CONFLICT

It seems obvious that benefits are to be gained if people manage conflict situations so as to keep the flow of communication between them and their adversary moving. Doing so may contribute to increased levels of mutual understanding and trust that can then slow and even halt the escalatory process. In the communicative interaction with the other, the adversary acquires a face, which renders the destruction of the other less likely, or at least more difficult, than when the opponent is a faceless enemy. Without information flows and exchanges, there is wide open space for unfounded rumors, distortions of information, and lies. Direct interaction between adversaries in a conflict situation can help parties to explain their motivations and actions, assist them to understand their respective sensitivities, and, thus, lead them toward acts that avoid unnecessarily angering the other parties. In this exchange, parties may also discover that the conflict is largely based on procedural issues that can be resolved through a discussion about mutual needs and priorities. Nevertheless, however important communication processes may be, they offer no guarantee that conflicts de-escalate.

Communication between parties in dispute is unlikely to support de-escalation if those parties are too angry with each other or feel too threatened. If there has been an earlier traumatic experience between the parties, communication is likely to fail. Communication is also problematic in situations of inequality. Between unequal partners, there is a strong likelihood that continued communication serves the stronger party better than the weaker party. In unequal marital relations, for example, the advice (given by marriage counselors) to continue to communicate is often very detrimental for the more dependent partner. He or she needs to dissociate from the relationship, even if only temporarily. He or she needs the space to self-empower and to gain a more autonomous position, which is impossible as long as they continue to engage in a communication process. The stronger party is too overbearing and leaves no space for independent thinking on the part of the weaker party. Dissociation is a process of deliberate withdrawal that allows one to create the silence in one's head that is essential to autonomous thought and choice.

Particularly in intergroup conflict, the intensification of communication between parties may strengthen the identification with the in-group and increase the hostility toward the out-group as the interaction easily transforms into mutual insulting and becomes an angry shouting match.

If parties to a conflict intend to use communication strategies in order to win, possible benefits are likely to evaporate. Being able to productively use communication will also depend on the context of the conflict situation. There are circumstances during which parties would do better not to communicate. For example, if there is any time pressure—if one needs to keep a deadline—a confrontational conversation will probably make the conflict worse. Parties should agree on a time when both can focus on the conflict issue.

In a stressful environment—the computer crashed, the car broke down, the kids vomited—the exchange about a marital conflict is usually disastrous. Parties are likely to say things (e.g., about "your mother") that have dramatic and lasting negative effects.

In order for communication to tame conflicts, there should be a communicative space in which parties can accept their vulnerability and uncertainty and, by doing so, diminish their subjective space. This will create more intersubjective space for listening and understanding each other.

Another consideration is that many daily conflicts are of a low complexity and can be solved by piecemeal approaches—that is, by dealing with misunderstandings, nuisances, and past happenings in a step-by-step manner. Group conflicts, however, are different, in that they are usually of a high complexity because they involve very divergent assumptions, expectations, and purposes. Most low-intensity conflicts can be resolved through mediation, clarification of misunderstandings, or win-win forms of accommodation. High-complexity conflicts, however, carry a large risk of escalation. Moreover, the escalation process prolongs the conflict, and its participants live increasingly with tunnel visions of the situation and their adversary. As Nelson Mandela remarked, "One effect of sustained conflicts is to narrow our vision of what is possible" (in Kahane, 2004, p. 41).

Once the "spiral of evil" sets in, the exercise of violence can often be brought under (temporary) control by external violent intervention, the victory of one of the battling parties (which evidently implies defeat for the other party—a fertile ground for more battle in the future), battle fatigue (resources may dry up), or well-intended projects of postconflict economic development that may replenish resources so the battling can go on.

In analyzing the role of communication in group conflicts, then, one should address the often overrated expectations of the provision of information. People generally believe that more and better information and more and open communication is essential for the prevention of escalation. The underlying assumption here is that once people know more about each other, they will understand each other better and be less inclined to behave violently toward each other.

Such assumptions deserve a skeptical assessment. They are largely valid only if one believes that conflicts and their escalation into violence are primarily caused by insufficient and inadequate information. From this reasoning, it follows that parties can control conflicts once adversaries have correct information about each other. This also suggests that if adversaries knew more about each other, they would find agreement easier to reach. It is, however, difficult to find empirical evidence for this and one can equally well propound the view that social harmony is largely due to the degree of ignorance that people have about each other. As a matter of fact, many societies maintain levels of stability because they employ rituals, customs, and conventions that enable their members to engage in social interaction without having detailed information about who they really are.

Consequently, these assumptions neglect the fact that conflicts often address very real points of contention. Conflicts may be very dangerous precisely because adversaries have full information about each other's aims and motives. In fact, more information about the adversary may actually lead to more conflict. For example, during the Cold War, a critical component in nuclear stability between the United States and the Soviet Union was that both powers lacked information about the exact location of the other's nuclear submarines. Because these weapons were difficult to detect, they likewise were difficult to target, and might escape a first strike and render a debilitating second strike to the attacker. The mutual ignorance about weapons' locations was a powerful deterrent against a first nuclear strike by either party.

Thus, complete informational openness may enhance conflict, and it could be argued that a functional level of secrecy contributes positively to societal security. A level of secrecy is also helpful in containing potential conflict escalation because it leaves ample space for face-saving disclaimers in critical negotiations.

Furthermore, in conflict situations, the problem is often one of an abundance rather than a dearth of information. In decision making, the flow of messages that needs to be evaluated may become dysfunctional once it reaches a critical mass. The overload may seriously impede rational decision making because the means of coping with it (such as selective filtering, stereotyping, and simplistic structuring) results in misperceptions and incorrect interpretations.

Another consideration comes from the UNESCO Constitution (1945), which states that war begins in the minds of people.[1] This suggests that the minds of people need to be influenced—through the media—in order to develop a culture of peace. However, the idea that war begins in people's minds is misleading. Wars start with the material, physical fact of their bodies. The human life form—like other life forms—is constantly involved in a struggle for life. Aggression and violence are inevitable components of that struggle. In such struggles, information campaigns directed at people's "hearts and minds" will do little to make conflicts less dangerous.

Another problem with properly informing the public about what happens in the world is the assumption that people are predominantly rational beings whose viewpoints are defined by new information and who, on the basis of new information, change earlier positions and develop new insights. Reality is different! People often know already—on emotional and irrational grounds—what they should think. They filter out information that does not match their expectations, and as a result, information that threatens to undermine their established opinions is simply discarded. People tend to believe that their assumptions are correct and do not need to be questioned. The idea that people would want information in order to arrive at better decisions is based on the assumption that processes of decision making proceed in orderly and rational ways. More often than not, however, social and personal decision making is a chaotic process driven by irrational and ad hoc motives. If human beings were rational and logical information-processing systems, they would more often change opinions and positions than they actually do.

PEACE JOURNALISM

Various authors have suggested a format in which communication could contribute to de-escalation: peace journalism. This notion was launched by Norwegian peace researcher Johan Galtung as a counterpoint to the dominant format of conflict reporting. Peace journalism has also been promoted by academic and journalist Jack Lynch at the Centre for Peace and Conflict Studies of the University of Sydney. On the one hand, conventional war journalism focuses on war as a zero-sum game with winners versus losers, is oriented toward us-versus-them propaganda, and uses victory and defeat metaphors. Peace journalism, on the other hand, is more empathic and proactive, and focuses on the effects of violence. It exposes propagandistic lies and highlights peace initiatives. In short, peace journalism provides more balanced news coverage; seeks alternative interpretations; focuses on context; is proactive; humanizes all sides in a conflict; exposes lies from all sides; depicts the suffering, pain, and trauma of warfare; and de-anonymizes adversaries. The key hypothesis of peace journalism studies is that "conventional news routines and news values tend towards conflict escalation" (Hackett & Schroeder, 2008, p. 26). Suleyman Irvan (2006) defined peace journalism as a normative theory that obliges media to be socially responsible and promote peace. In other words, peace journalism proposes what media should do in order to positively contribute to preventing violent conflict.

The literature on peace journalism is aware of essential obstacles that stand in the way of realizing this normative position. For example, conceptions of journalistic professionalism, ideas about news values, and objectivity can impede peace journalism's aim because calling on these ideals suggests that peace journalism threatens professional integrity and independent reporting of the news. There are also institutional impediments to peace journalism, such as prevailing mode of organiza-tion and the management of media that often operate as commercial enterprises driven by an obsession with market shares, ratings, and scoops. Nationalist sentiments also form obstacles. When the nation goes to war, the media are strongly inclined to follow the flag and become partisan to the conflict.

Overall, the main question would not seem to be whether a peace journalism format could be helpful to de-escalate conflict. It is pretty obvious that within reasonable limits, a more balanced and less propa-gandistic, partisan, and war-triumphalist news reporting provides for more serious questioning of the dangers of conflict escalation. It may also stimulate the uncritical bystanders in conflict situations to ask more questions. However, an important task for peace journalism could be to go beyond the focus on reporting present conflict and to also address issues of postescalation situations.

HUMAN RIGHTS REPARATIONS

Parties that engage in violent conflict should be made aware of the long-term responsibilities that conflict escalation may imply. There is a tendency among governments and citizens of countries that go to war (like the military actions in Iraq and Afghanistan) to ignore warring na-tions' responsibility for the victims that war creates. The reality of any war, regardless of whatever one thinks about its (il)legitimacy, is that innocent men, women, and children are wounded, mutilated, killed, or traumatized, and that all these victims have loved ones who suffer tremendously. Media could play an essential role to raise awareness about our responsibilities for the victims we make. For years, well-known human rights scholars such as Theo van Boven[2] have already been working toward a system of repair payments to the victims of gross human rights violations.

In media reports on Guantánamo Bay, the emphasis in 2009 was focused on the decision by U.S. president Obama to close the U.S. prison in Cuba. In 2010 there was still little clarity about what would happen next. Whatever happens, it is likely that a majority of the prisoners will turn out be innocent, as in the case of Sami al-Haj, the Al Jazeera cameraman who was kept in prison for six years and who, during that time, was humiliated and beaten. He was later released after being found innocent. The U.S. government made a mistake, and now that Sami al-Haj is back in the Sudan, he says he feels alienated from his wife and his son and is no longer able to make jokes. He is free, but how can he get his sense of humor back? All those who were complicit in the crimes perpetrated against him cannot give the jokes back to him, but they at least are responsible for repair payments. In a fair and just international system of governance, belligerent governments would face enormous demands for repair payments from Iraqi and Afghan citizens or from Palestinian citizens in the Gaza strip. In this way, news media around the world could make people aware that if they support warfare, they have to accept the responsibility for all the victims they create. Media could teach people to understand that there are no "clean" wars.

For postescalation situations in which parties want to prevent another spiral of escalation, the experience of collaboratively designing future scenarios offers a promising venue that could reach out to audiences worldwide through news media. If the prevention of conflict escalation has failed, then the prime concern becomes the healing of the pain, losses, physical and mental mutilations, and scars that remain.

THE MONT FLEUR EXPERIENCE

Postescalation healing requires a holistic, future-oriented, and partici-patory approach. The South African experience with the Mont Fleur scenario project could help guide us to such an approach.

In 1991 a scenario project began in South Africa as part of the tran-sition process from the apartheid regime to an egalitarian, democratic regime. The first workshop of the project took place with twenty-two influential South Africans in the Mont Fleur Conference Centre on a wine estate outside Cape Town. Adam Kahane (2004), who worked at the time for Shell Oil Company, introduced the Shell scenario method to the participants and asked them to use the Shell convention to talk not about what they wanted to happen but about what might happen regardless of what they wanted. Kahane reported that "Each small group could present back to the whole group any story they wanted, as long as they could argue that it was logical and plausible.... The team found this scenario game fabulously liberating" (2004, p. 21).

Then, in a final workshop in 1992, the participants designed four sce-narios for public debate. The leading question was, "How will the South African transition go, and will the country succeed in 'taking off'? Each of the four stories gave a different answer and had a different message that mattered to the country in 1992" (Kahane, 2004, p. 22).

Reflecting later on the experience of these workshops, Kahane commented,

The essence of the Mont Fleur process, I saw, was that a small group of deeply committed leaders, representing a cross-section of a society that the whole world considered irretrievably stuck, had sat down to-gether to talk broadly and profoundly about what was going on and what should be done. More than that, they had not talked about what other people—some faceless authorities or decision makers—should do to advance some parochial agenda, but what they and their colleagues and their fellow citizens had to do in order to create a better future for everybody. They saw themselves as part of—not apart from—the prob-lem they were trying to solve. The scenarios were a novel means to this engaged problem-solving end. (2004, p. 26)

This project, therefore, used the scenario approach not only to un-derstand the historical process but also to shape it. Kahane cited Joseph Jaworski, author of *Synchronicity: The Inner Path of Leadership,* who wrote, "Using scenarios in this way can be an extraordinarily powerful process—helping people to sense and actualise emerging new realities" (2004, p. 27). Kahane then went on to observe, "Everywhere ... people are struggling to find peaceful ways to solve their own highly complex problems. The lessons of the South African transition and of Mont Fleur are therefore relevant to many other countries" (p. 33).

It would seem—on the basis of experiences with student groups around the world[3]—that the Mont Fleur experience is exceptionally well suited to help people in postescalation situations talk to each other and design new futures in a nonthreatening and playful ambiance. What's more, media around the world could play a significant role in publicizing such experiences and demonstrating their effectiveness. In fact, using today's advanced communication and information technologies, media could offer platforms for groups participating in the exercise without necessarily being all physically present in the same venue.

What happens to the participants in Mont Fleur–type workshops needs to be extended to societies at large. Doing so requires, among other factors, the collaboration of mass media. This is difficult given either the reservations that media producers (and certainly journalists) entertain against their involvement in societal projects, which they tend to perceive as challenges to their professional autonomy, or—and more dangerously—the manipulation of media by myopic, self-centered po-litical agendas.

If media claim—as they often do—that they are neutral, their op-erational logic will render them accomplices to conflict escalation. The ultimate question is, if one wants to stay an outsider in between groups, can one also remain neutral to the question of whether societies will experience escalating or de-escalating evil?

The Mont Fleur approach could also be used in the pre-escalation phase of high-complexity conflicts. During this phase, those aware of the risk of escalating conflict should try to get the groups involved together to design scenarios for their future coexistence. Again, rather than further disconnecting conflicting parties, media could make a public effort to bring them together in a project that is novel to all concerned. Mass media can demonstrate the potential of this approach by broadly disseminating information about it, showing successful cases, and, thus, stimulating people to participate.

BEYOND PEACE JOURNALISM

However relevant all this may be, there are also serious flaws in the peace journalism proposals. On the substantial level, it would seem that the notion of "peace" belongs too much to the romantic, idealist repertoire to be useful. It is highly unlikely that the reality, pervasiveness, and perseverance of intergroup conflicts can be transformed into sustainable peaceful relations. Thus, the present study focuses instead on preventing conflict escalation. Although this may seem a minimal goal, in reality, it is incredibly difficult to achieve: Too much historical evidence supports Reinhold Niebuhr's conclusion that "society is in a perpetual state of war" (1932, p. 19) to expect journalists to be able to promote peace.

Chapters 4, 5, and 7 will address a more limited approach to "media and conflict" that is largely inspired by the second flaw in peace journalism proposals: the lack of awareness of the necessity of societal receptivity to the offerings of the peace-promoting journalist. Unless societies (i.e., media audiences) at large care about the specific qualities of more qualified, more contextualized, less sensationalist, less partisan, and more investigative conflict reporting, the peace journalistic effort is an exercise in futility. As suggested before, an essential question is whether the realities of news production as business, of news as commodity, and of prevailing news-institutional interests and professional standard operations can accommodate the routines and value orientations of media formats that accommodate peace journalism in both pre- and postescalation situations. This would definitely require a substantial change in the ways journalism is organized on the supply side. Even more importantly, though, this requires—on the demand side—a substantial change in news audiences' expectations. Critical researchers may propose different news styles, but global audiences in massive numbers demonstrate no dissatisfaction with the "news as it is."

Accordingly, the concern for mass media performance is not the sole responsibility of media producers. It also involves client communities. In 1969 Wilbur Schramm and William L. Rivers wrote, "The listening, viewing, reading public underestimates its power," arguing that public regulatory bodies, the media themselves, and the general public share responsibility for the quality of mass communication (p. 249). In 1993 journalist Mort Rosenblum also included the role of the general public in the inadequacies of international news reporting, stating, "If the suppliers haven't done better, it is because consumers have not demanded it" (p. 287).

When armed conflicts begin, one often hears the words of Senator Hiram Johnson: "The first casualty when war comes is the truth."[4] But a probable second victim would seem to be the public interest in knowing the truth. Often media audiences prefer not to know all the details of armed confrontations. Reliable media need good-quality audiences. Because the provision of information is of critical importance in democratic societies, citizens can be asked to be vigilant media consumers who actively and critically reflect on media contents. Unless media consumers worldwide demand to be properly informed about conflicts in peace journalism formats, it is unrealistic to expect the news business to change winning horses. Media are part of the societal context within which they function. The more this context opens possibilities for people to address anxieties, resist agitation, and withstand disconnectedness from others, the better the media potential for helping to de-escalate conflicts will develop. This obviously implies a position about the media-society relationship. Research evidence does indeed suggest that, by and large, media are followers and not leaders. In most important social debates, whereas media may appear to be the initiators, they are, in fact, usually the disseminators—the amplifiers—not the pioneers. Examples abound of political groups, activists, and religious movements that are the first definers of social issues such as gender, race, pacifism, or climate change.

It is possible to identify three crucial societal mechanisms that may promote de-escalatory processes and to which media could make significant contributions:

1. learning "mindful" communication that creates the intersubjective space for speaking openly, listening actively, and stepping out of

the mental cages from which so much human communication is conducted;

2. creating communicative spaces where people can engage in "disarming" conversation; and

3. establishing an early warning system that signals in time the beginnings of public incitement to humiliation and massacre.

NEW MEDIA

Because so far much attention was given to "conventional" media and their role in relation to conflict, the reader may wonder what happened to the "new" media? Do the new possibilities of the Internet, and especially of Web 2.0—weblogging, Facebook and other social networking sites, hyves, and YouTube and other social broadcasting sites—along with mobile phone message systems expand human communications' capacity to the extent that new ways of coping with conflict are created?

Firstly, the new media are not by any standard free of conflict. Today, for example, the Internet has become a virtual battlefield for religious conflict. There is a disconcertingly large volume of hate speech related to sexism and racism. There is xenophobic and homophobic speech. Apparently, e-mail has also been discovered as a convenient medium for death threats. Across the world, SMS messages are used to incite hate and violence.

Secondly, the notion of "new" suggests not only advances in information and communication technology but also changes in human behavior. This does, however, reflect a crude determinism that finds no substance in human realities. If people cannot or do not want to master the skills of mindful communication (which are not part of the human) regardless of whatever new tools they use, their mode of communication will do nothing to tame the spiral of escalation.

Thirdly, the "new" media may be free from oligopolistic control by the barons of culture, the moguls that gatekeep the news, or the few that belong to a ruling class, an aristocratic elite, or a religious priesthood. The new media may have the masses at the helm. There is, however, no historical evidence to suggest that the masses will be less inclined than the few to the escalation of conflict.

Fourthly, the "new" media may indeed bring about more freedom to foster, express, disseminate, and receive ideas, but there is no guarantee that the largely expanded and differentiated number of media producers will act more responsibly than the media moguls of the past.

Lastly, how far the conventional mass media are now past history remains to be seen. Today, they continue to be grand players in the global facilitation and dissemination of anxiety, agitation, alienation, and mirrored accusations.

CONCLUSION

In this chapter, I argued that de-escalating the spiral of conflict demands new forms of journalism such as peace journalism. However, no matter how helpful such departures from conventional news reporting may be, they nonetheless stay within the boundaries of "old" and "new" media. In order to de-escalate conflict, a crucial requirement for parties to a conflict is, first of all, the learning of a mode of mindful communication that will be proposed in the next chapter.

CHAPTER **4**

MINDFUL COMMUNICATION

⊸

MINDFULNESS

The concept "mindfulness" constitutes the core of Buddhist psychology. Its essential components are awareness, attention, and acceptance. As Christopher Germer wrote,

> To be mindful is to wake up, to recognize what is happening in the present moment. We are rarely mindful. We are usually caught up in distracting thoughts or in opinions about what is happening in the moment. This is mindlessness. (Germer, Siegel, & Fulton, 2005, pp. 4–5)

Thus, being mindful means that we are aware of ourselves and our environment in a nonjudgmental way. Attention means we are no longer preoccupied with the past or the future: The attention is on the present. We do not know what will be next and are able to concede that we do not know, and that we cannot control it. Acceptance is the willingness to let things be as they are at the moment.

In dealing with physical pain, for example, we become aware of the pain, pay attention to it, and accept it. The conventional treatment of pain focuses on pain relief, such as pharmaceutical painkillers do.

However, only if one accepts pain can there truly be recovery from pain. The effort to alleviate pain makes the suffering only worse. Mindfulness is a skill that can be learned and has been effectively applied in psychotherapy and pain relief.

Mindless speech is speaking without really thinking. Mindless speech means that one communicates on autopilot. Many people experience this with e-mail communications. How often would it have been better if the message had not been sent so quickly! When one conducts actions without attention, realizing what has happened usually comes too late. One begins eating small snacks at a reception party, and before long, the bowl of nuts is empty and the diet ruined. Mindless eating, like mindless speech, is a tremendous waste of energy and can be hurtful for both oneself and others. People are often deeply hurt by remarks made in a mindless, cavalier fashion.

Mindless speech is, to use a phrase from Germer, Siegel, and Fulton (2005, p. 5), like "snacking without being aware of eating."

Mindful speech is speaking with concentrated attention. The mindful person tastes the food and does not swallow it mindlessly. Mindful speakers use words with prudence because they realize that words can be weapons that are thus capable of enormous destruction. This prudence creates space for de-escalating conflict.

Mindful speech is a mode of conversation that is in the present. Engaging in mindful speech is difficult because we are often preoccupied during conversations with thoughts about the past and the future. In mindful speech, however, there is an awareness of conversing with the other, there is attention to whom one converses with, to what is said as well as what is nonverbally communicated. There is acceptance, which means that we let the conversation be as it is. This may involve negative and unpleasant emotions, but the experience is as it is; we cannot change the experience. If we feel this is unpleasant or even painful, we have to admit this and accept it rather than frantically try to relieve the displeasure. Recognizing the unpleasantness of a conversation will bring a good chance of freeing oneself from it.

Mindfulness in communication means that we live the moment of communication. We taste the words, feel the texture of our language, notice the warmth or lack thereof in the conversation, discover the minute changes in speech. We ask ourselves what is happening in the interaction with others. We accept the power of communicative silence but also notice when its quality changes from the experience of communion to a lack of interest.

In this chapter, I propose that nurturing mindfulness in communication may contribute to taming the spiral of escalation. It may be an essential element in a de-escalatory mode of communicating. To achieve this is a tall order indeed because in so many human communication processes—particularly those mediated by news and entertainment in the mass media—"mindlessness" prevails over "mindfulness."

Human communication has different faces. The notion of faces of communication is borrowed from Kenneth Boulding's book *Three Faces of Power* (1990). In his impressive study on power, Boulding analyzed its three faces: the destructive, the productive, and the integrative faces of power. In a similar way, one could think of the different faces of communication and distinguish the destructive-mindless and escalatory face versus the integrative-mindful and de-escalatory face of human communication. It is interesting to note here that Boulding argued that historically, productive and integrative power are more decisive than destructive power (1990, pp. 226–227), which leads us to ask whether the same may be true for communication.

The Modalities of Mindless Versus Mindful Communication

The different modalities of mindless versus mindful communication are:

Mindless Communication	Mindful Communication
Absolutist	Reflexive
Violent	Nonviolent
Aggressive	Assertive
Deficit	Swap
Polemical	Dialogical
Instrumental	Relational
Synchronic	Diachronic

These modalities can be described as follows:

Absolutist Speech

Absolutist speech gives more space to subjectivity than to intersubjectivity. The speaker's "Fat Ego" (Kunneman, 2005) stands in the way of recognizing what others have to say. He/she speaks with certainty. There is a frequent use of statements like "I know" and "There can be no doubt." For the absolutist speaker, there is no need to ask questions.

Absolutist speech is abundantly present in politics. Very telling illustrations come from political speech in connection with the military invasion of Iraq. Speeches by U.S. president Bush and Vice President Cheney were full of statements like "we know with absolute certainty" or "there is no doubt." Moreover, their political discourse identified uncertainty and hesitation as a dangerous mindset. The absolutist speech is dogmatic, which in itself angers other parties in a dispute. When, subsequently, what was presented as a known fact turns out to be wrong, the speaker comes under fire and is exposed as a fool. When the dogmatic speaker tries to save face by overpowering the critic with rhetorical or even physical violence, the conflict escalates.

Absolutist speech has a particularly strong appeal in times of uncertainty and fear. The absolutist accepts only his own truth and has a mission that tolerates no opposition. Dissidents are heretics who should preferably burn at the stake. The absolutist mode of speech spreads like bushfire through the Internet as hate sites and Web sites with extremism, nationalism, revisionism, and racism proliferate.

Reflexive Speech

Reflexive speech is capable of admitting uncertainty. It reflects a skeptical attitude about such notions as truth and certainty. It uses expressions like "I believe," "I feel," or even "I am confident." Thus, there remains space for revision and correction. Errors can be afforded and earlier statements can be taken back without serious loss of face. Even if statements are made with confidence but not with absolute certainty, the speaker is likely to feel less embarrassed and foolish when those statements are found to be wrong. The criticism is likely to be less severe and more accommodating. The speaker's nondogmatic and open mind makes de-escalation possible.

Violent Speech

Violent speech is judgmental. The speaker has ready labels for other parties: They are lazy, unreliable, stupid, or even evil. Such labels amount to moral judgments that assume that the speaker knows what is right and wrong and is able to put the other's wrong right. Labels limit perceptions of others and obstruct seeing the whole person. The speaker does not notice how his speech affects others and how his implied judgments (which are often denunciations) evoke resistance and violence on the part of those he speaks to or about. Violent speech refuses to show vulnerability. It never asks what the needs of others may be. Violent speech locks people up into the categories that others then use to define them. It imposes demands on others that are expressed in ways that imply (threats of) sanctions if they don't comply.

Nonviolent Speech

Nonviolent speech is empathic. In the famous dialogue between Carl Rogers and Martin Buber, Rogers saw empathy as understanding someone else's life from the other's perspective. Conversely, to Buber it meant inclusion of the other so one could experience the other side (Cissna & Anderson, 1998). Either way, empathy is based on looking at others without judgment. As German singer Ruth Bebermeyer tells us in a touching song, "I never saw a dumb kid but I did see a kid that did things I did not understand" (Rosenberg, 2003, p. 20).

The nonviolent speaker is ready to express feelings, doubts, and uncertainties. Concerns are not expressed as demands but instead as genuine questions.

Aggressive Speech

Aggressive speech is a communications mode in which people defend their own interests without reckoning with others. Aggressive speech imposes, unilaterally, solutions onto others and gives them no choice. It excludes others and denies them communicative space. It is often combined with intimidating body language and a loud voice.

Assertive Speech

Assertive speech means that people stand up for their rights while still respecting other people's rights. Nonassertive communication, in which one effaces oneself, appears noble but is in actuality very confrontational for others because the speaker constantly thinks about what others may find. It is more helpful to let others know what you think and want rather than inviting them to engage in guesswork. Doing so leaves sufficient space for others to present their views and preferences. Assertive communication means that parties balance their space with the other's space. The assertive speaker shares responsibility for possible solutions to disputes by giving others a choice. Assertive speech is about engaging with others, acknowledging the reality of the other, not relinquishing one's own ground, and yet remaining open to change in the relationship (Cissna & Anderson, 1998, p. 92).

Assertive speech is not the same as polite speech. This is saying what the speaker assumes other individuals want to hear (Kahane, 2004, pp. 56–57).

Deficit Speech

Deficit speech is based on the assumption of deficits in other people. The speaker thinks the addressed party lacks knowledge, understanding, or capability, and this needs to be repaired by the speaker. Deficit speech is persuasive communication; it tells others what they need to know, but this speech tells it many times over with increasing force, volume, and then with the threat of sanctions.

Deficit speech takes as its starting point the inequalities among the parties involved. As a result, it does not recognize the other as a person in his/her own right.

Swap Speech

Swap speech is based on the notion of barter trade. It starts from the assumption that all parties involved can offer contributions and that all also have deficits. The speaker accepts that communication is a co-learning process. In swap speech, all parties change and—in the end—are better off.

Polemical Speech

It is often argued that politics needs polemics and that the clash of opinions leads to the discovery of the truth. In reality, however, clashes usually lead to more misery than truth. Polemics is not without risk. It is verbal combat, a form of rhetorical war. It uses words as weapons, which manifests violence. Verbal violence can cause great damage and even lead to physical violence. It is, for example, not without danger to describe enemies as fascists or terrorists. Deploying words as weapons starts a spiral that easily ends with using weapons as words. Furthermore, media tend to give disproportional dimensions to polemical debates.

This may be spectacular entertainment but seldom serves substantial purposes. In media debates, participants tend to not listen and to use pseudo-arguments, sophisms, and references to uncontrollable sources. The debate is a sequence of monologues, a battle of one-liners that reduce realities to oversimplifications.

In most media around the world, debate is a very popular format whereas the opportunities for genuine dialogue tend to be minimal.

Dialogical Speech

Dialogical speech confronts parties with the difficult art of listening and questioning pet theories and beloved assumptions. A meaningful dialogue begins with an internal dialogue. This means that all participants question their own judgments and assumptions. Critically investigating our own assumptions is, however, a major challenge because we are often ignorant about our basic assumptions. Assumptions are the mental maps that we tend to follow uncritically. We all have different and often conflicting assumptions, and this is certainly the case when we come from different cultures. Furthermore, suspending judgment is equally difficult because we are strongly attached to our opinions and assessments and prefer them to uncertainties.

Carl Rogers and Martin Buber took their dialogue seriously, as "They recognized in unprecedented ways the importance of careful and thoughtful listening" (Cissna & Anderson, 1998, p. 92). Active listening means that people admit they do not have the truth because knowing what is true makes listening superfluous. Active listening empowers the people who are listened to, allowing them to discover new choices and new possibilities. People often know what they can do but because nobody ever listens, they do not take their own potential seriously. Active listening also implies that people listen to each other not merely in a defensive way in order to be prepared for rebuttal; they also listen with empathy and reflexivity in order to be able to see reality from a different perspective. Learning the language of listening is very hard in societies that are increasingly influenced by visual cultures whereas listening demands an ear-centered culture. Most of the mass media offer their audiences "talk shows," but no "listening shows."

Dialogic speech requires participants to recognize the significance of silence—not in the sense of withholding, but as the constructive rests that are used in musical compositions. The dialogue can only take place when silence is respected. This borders on the impossible in modern societies, where talking never seems to stop and where every void needs to be filled. In genuine dialogic speech, the parties also recognize that they are different. In doing so, they accept the "otherness of the other."

In most societies people have neither time nor patience for dialogical speech. Dialogues have no short-term or certain outcomes. This conflicts with the spirit of modern achievement-oriented societies. Conducting a dialogue is a demanding art that needs to be learned. In many societies, people have neither the time nor the patience for dialogical communication. Moreover, the mass media are not particularly helpful in teaching people the art of conversation. Much of their content is babbling (endless talking without saying anything), advertising blurbs, sound-bites, or polemical debate.

Instrumental Speech

Instrumental speech means that the speaker uses communication in an instrumental way, to serve his personal interests or the interests of the group to which he belongs. In instrumental communication, the other is used as a means. The significance of the other is judged in terms of his relative usefulness to achieve "our" goals. In many daily interactions, people "instrumentalize" each other, thereby imposing on others their definitions of their own and others' identities.

Relational Speech

Relational speech refers to interactions in which others are seen as unique individuals with faces, stories, and experiences. In relational speech, others are goals and not instruments. Through relational speech, the speaker wants to understand who the other is—even if the other is labeled a "terrorist."

Relational speech implies that people do not just talk *to* others but actually talk *with* each other. In this interaction, they feel free to say what they think and, thus, they have the courage to speak up. In relational speech, people provide others with the space to be themselves. Herewith, they surrender their need to have control over others.

Synchronic Speech

In the synchronic mode of communication, people are synchronized with the definitions they themselves and others have created for their identity. Synchronic speech is essentialist: Once your identity is defined, this is your essence ("who you really are"), which will not change.

Therefore, the synchronic speaker also knows what others think, want, and feel. A common expression in synchronic speech is "I know what you are thinking." This is a type of mind reading that has pushed many holiday-dinner disputes into the danger zone! The synchronic speaker is not open to learning about others; rather, he would try to synchronize their thinking to become like his.

Diachronic Speech

Diachronic literally means "through time." Thus, it refers to the "historization" of interactions and puts them in the context of processes of development. Basic to the notion is that there is always change and development in situations of human encounter. Cratylus, a student of Greek philosopher Heraclitus (535–475 B.C.), illustrated this when he observed that a person never steps twice in the same river. The next time the water is different; the river is not the same. Applied to human communication, this means that you never speak twice with the same person. In diachronic speech, the partners in encounters should not be tied to who they were yesterday because they are people who are constantly changing and growing.

TRAINING

These different modes of speech raise the question of whether humans can change from "mindless" to "mindful" communicators. In training sessions on different modes of communication, people can certainly be made aware of how mindless communication escalates conflict and how mindful communication can help de-escalate conflict. Among the comments that participants in such seminars made, the following is very characteristic of their experiences:

It was amazing for me to see how the image of a person is influenced by his acting within a dispute or a conflict. In the first turn, there were a lot of negative feelings towards each opponent, which also the bystanders could notice. And just by changing the behavior, everybody is able to de-escalate such difficult and dangerous situations as we saw and did in the second turn. When I was sitting in front of the class and playing the role of the closed person who is not willing to cooperate, I felt very strange because I had to present an attitude which is contrary to mine. But it was not so bad due to the fact that every participant had to play this role. This Case Study showed me the background of escalating situations and that it's possible to de-escalate them with the right behavior. And it was very interesting to feel what people feel within a conflict which probably escalates.[1]

In formal and informal education—in institutions such as schools, universities, churches, mosques, companies, and hospitals—there are ample opportunities to learn from existential confrontations with mindless versus mindful modes of communication.

CHILDREN

There is no better way to work on the social transformation from mindless to mindful communication than to begin to create opportunities for "mindful" communication with children. An important way to give children the ability to develop and share their questions and observations is to give them access to the media. Actually, Article 13 of the Convention on the Rights of Children provides children's right of access to the media and, thus, suggests that there should be more children's voices in the media.[2] If one puts this within the context of the essential human rights standard of human equality, this means that children around the world should have equal opportunity to access communication media. From this perspective, the current global digital divide—between and within countries—has serious implications for children. The bridging of the divide is especially urgent in view of the future participation in knowledge societies by young people.

In a conference to discuss implementing the Children's Convention (the Oslo Challenge), participants proposed that children should learn as much as they can about the media "so that they can make informed choices as media consumers and gain maximum benefit from the diversity the media offer."[3] The Oslo meeting also challenges children "to grasp opportunities to participate in production of media output." Presently, around the world there is a growing number of good practices that demonstrate how children can contribute to media production.[4] Illustrative examples come from a wide range of projects, from the Young Reporters of Albania, who are responsible for selecting stories and planning TV production, to "Our Own Voice" in Haiti, which empowers child journalists, to street-level youth media in Chicago that educates inner-city youth in media arts, to the Free News project in Bangladesh that trains young journalists and provides a model of opportunities for child participation in the media, to the French Journalist for a Day event, which provides young people with a chance to participate in a real in-house newspaper enterprise.

The realization of children's participation in media production is a tall order because it often confronts such obstacles as the child-unfriendly work culture in many media institutions, the absence of appropriate facilities, and inadequate safety measures. Creating children's media does not by itself guarantee that their productions use de-escalatory modes of communication. In order to achieve this, another requirement would need to be met: the openness in educational programs to help ease the transition from "mindless" to "mindful" communication. There are impressive examples of pedagogical projects where children are exposed to de-escalatory interaction, such as the Reggio Emilia project.[5]

A basic insight of this project is that children have 100 languages and that they want to use them all. Children talk in all these languages and have always done so, but in most forms of education (at home and in school), their voices have been censored away. In Reggio Emilia, these voices are listened to because children see worlds and meanings that adults have forgotten. In most educational projects, 99 of the 100 languages will be stolen from the kids. Among those is the language of asking questions. Most of the world's educational programs conform to the Platonic proposition that intelligence is measured by the capacity to respond to questions. This is what is routinely applied in higher education, such as at universities or in the very popular TV science quizzes. The suggestion that science equals finding smart answers to questions is very detrimental for developing creative and critical thinking. Against the Platonic position, there is a different philosophical tradition that measures intelligence by the capacity to ask questions. Reggio Emilia allows children to have questions and uncertainties and, thus, to develop their own visions and dreams about the world. It familiarizes children with the insight that even the toughest conflicts in life are rarely choices between only two options, and it helps them to discover that there are always more choices available. Dilemmas become trilemmas, pentalemmas, or octolemmas! If we want to take away the roots of violence, move away from forms of war on terror that lead to even more violence, and develop ways of reporting that make critical reflection possible, we should begin by giving the kids of the world their hundred languages and their hundred dreams back.

Music Teaching

Arguably the most promising format to help children learn "mindful" communication is through teaching music. In Paris, one finds in the

Rue Saint-Jacques the Ecole Supérieure de Musique, Danse, et d'Art Dramatique. Artists such as Satie, Debussy, Albéniz, and Messiaen all taught there, and Cole Porter studied there. This imaginative school, which began as Schola Cantorum, genuinely cares for music. It renounces competition. Its basic philosophy is "On ne fait pas de musique contre quelqu'un" (One does not make music against someone else) (Carhart, 2002, p. 174).

This is an inspirational statement that can be adjusted for learning about communication: People do not communicate against each other but with each other. The Portuguese piano virtuoso Maria Pires practices this counsel in her own music education. For her, learning to play music is an adventurous exploration rather than an effort to impress parents and teachers. Because of the competitive drive in many conservatories around the world, most musical education is fine for highly motivated and talented children but does little to develop motivation and talent for all the others. Pires wants her students to discover the fun in music and the love for music, and she discourages them from participating in music contests. She contends that the competitive drive stands in the way of really listening to the music and cooperating with others. Furthermore, one of the grand old men of jazz music, (late) pianist Hank Jones, once said after a concert, "I never compete with fellow musicians, I only try to play better than I did yesterday and I do this by listening to the others, particularly the young ones."[6]

Therefore, music education can lay the foundation for "mindful" communication. It can teach kids to work together, enjoy cooperation, and listen to each other. In January 2003 Berliner Philharmoniker and its conductor Sir Simon Rattle helped realize a remarkable project in communication education through music and dance. With some 250 children between the ages of 7 and 30 from 25 different nationalities coming out of four Berlin schools, a performance of Stravinsky's *Le Sacre du Printemps* was given. Most of the dancers had never danced, were not familiar with classical music, and did not know each other. The project turned out to be a major experience in cross-cultural "mindful" communication. The children interacted with each other through music and dance. They learned to listen and to cooperate in an open-minded way.[7]

All this training and education will only make a broad societal impact if there is an environment that enables individuals and groups (such as the city dwellers that are central in the next chapter) to practice mindful communication.

ENABLING ENVIRONMENT

Mindful communication needs an environment that enables people to apply its essential modalities. An important aspect of such an environment is that the confidentiality of people's conversations is adequately secure. For people to really speak up and talk with others about their thoughts, they need to feel secure. This means that people need to be able to trust that their interactions are not monitored by third parties. Thus, under conditions of global surveillance, as Armand Mattelart has described (2008), people are not enabled to realize mindful communication. National measures, such as the U.S. Patriot Act, and international instruments, such as the surveillance network Echelon, create a social climate that discourages people from speaking freely.[8]

Mindful communication needs inclusiveness. This implies, among other things, that deaf people should have adequate access to the use of sign language or that there should be sufficient language provisions for migrant communities. In these communities, people need the linguistic capacity to converse both with the dominant culture of their new homeland and with the people of their own "roots." Inclusivity also affects people in mental institutions and prisons, and in many societies both the elderly and the young, who are often excluded from public conversation.

Mindful communication requires public space. This is a serious problem in societies in which the "privatization fever" transforms formerly public spaces into privately owned properties. What used to be the public marketplace has now often become the modern shopping mall, where privately hired guards control people's expressions and movements.

Mindful communication needs an environment in which people are being listened to. In many so-called democratic societies, people frequently feel that they are not taken seriously. Actually, ignoring people's voices has become widespread and has created around the world a tremendous loss of trust in the political system. There is a pervasive feeling among electorates in democracies that it does not matter what you say—you will not be heard.

CONCLUSION

Although the title of this book is *Media and Conflict,* the conclusion is that for the mass media to play a facilitating role in preventing conflict escalation, their primary focus should not be on themselves. The core concern should rather be developing a societal environment within which media can be realistically expected to employ de-escalatory modes of communication. One of the most important social environments in contemporary life is that of the city, to which the following chapter turns.

CHAPTER 5

THE COMMUNICATIVE CITY

On a cold January morning, a man played the violin in a Washington, D.C. metro station. He played during rush hour, when a large number of people passed while on their way to work. For about forty-five minutes, he played six pieces composed by Bach. Only a few people stopped and listened briefly; about twenty people gave money. He collected $32. When he finished, no one applauded. The only ones who noticed something remarkable was happening were some children who stopped to listen before their parents pushed them onward. This violinist was the world-famous musician Joshua Bell, who, the night before, had played for a jam-packed theater in Boston, with seats averaging $100 each. The Joshua Bell story suggests that the modern urban context is not receptive to the most pervasive mode of human communication across the borders of culture, religion, and ethnic origin: music. This raises the question of whether urbanites can communicate at all.

For the first time in history, humans will become the "urban species." In the years to come, some 70% of humanity will live in cities and many of these urban spaces will be megacities. This means that within these spaces, people will have to find ways to live together and to deal with the conflicts this implies. The quality and sustainability of life in the city will largely depend on the ways in which the urbanites manage to communicate with each other. Will there be willingness, capacity, and facilities to render the cities "communicative spaces"?

The concept of a "communicative city"[1] is based on the assumption that the way in which physical urban space is designed and developed will play a crucial role in determining whether the city offers human communicative space.

As was argued before, conflict is not inherently negative. All processes of change involve conflict. The real focus should, therefore, be on identifying creative forms of conflict management that keep the inevitable conflict within a safety zone. The danger is not in the conflict itself but rather in its escalation to dangerous and violent levels. In conflict management, preventive action is essential. Too often interventions and mediations take place when it is much too late and when too much damage has already been done. Consequently, the key question is, how can the escalation from low-intensity urban conflict to high-intensity urban conflict be prevented? A provisional answer may be found in addressing the quality of urban communication.

DISARMING CONVERSATION

Often urban communication is understood as the provision of information to urban dwellers, and this aspect of communication is undoubtedly very important. Certainly in democratically governed cities, citizens need to be well informed about urban matters. Moreover, citizens need to be regularly consulted through the voting polls, local referenda, or public hearings (Castells, 1991). However, even if this is all done in very satisfactory ways, the city may not necessarily be a "communicative city." The "communicative city" is a place that invites its inhabitants and its guests to interact with each other in "disarming conversation." This type of urban conversation is essential to the prevention of conflictual encounters escalating into violent conflicts. "Disarming conversation" is an approach to human interaction that keeps the spiral of escalation under control.

In urban space, people interact in myriad ways—often fleetingly, anonymously, nonverbally—and such encounters can be inspirational (stimulating our fantasies—"what if I had said something to her?"), absolutely insignificant, comforting (the consolatory effect of a friendly smile or the familiarity of a person one routinely sees), irritating, unnerving, and even intimidating. Some interactions have an intended or unintended physical component, which can be desirable or undesirable. One form of human interaction is conversation. This could take many different forms. Conversation can be an informative exchange, such as a simple question-and-answer session about where to find the post office. It can also be small talk about the weather or the misery of public transportation while waiting for the bus. It can also be a nasty dispute about perceived misconduct of other inhabitants of urban space.

The type of interaction that would seem crucial to conflict de-escalation could be described as "disarming conversation." This concept has been chosen because many people enter urban space heavily armed with what Goffman called "civil inattention" (1963). People are prepared to avoid others by using a body language that keeps others at a distance. They glance at others but see no faces (much like in dreams). They often bring expanded egos (this is *my* space) or fearful minds to urban in-teractivity. They are ready for combat. They may want peace, but they follow the old Roman dictum that advises if you want peace, prepare for war (Si vis pacem, para bellum). They have not yet learned the lesson from the peace movement that if you want peace, you should prepare for peace (Si vis pacem, para pacem). In order to engage in peaceful urban interaction—or at least to prevent encounters from spiraling into violence—city dwellers need to prepare for disarming conversation. This is the kind of exchange in which people feel they are taken seriously, in which they see the other as a "face," accept the "alterity" of the other as nonthreatening, learn from the encounter, and experience the joy of co-creative, "out of the box" thinking, in which conflicts become opportunities with many more options than the limited choices that initially restrained the interacting parties.

Most disputes in which people engage take the form of the classical dilemma: a difficult, sometimes impossible choice between two options. In the disarming conversation, people discover that most conflict situations in fact offer choices among a surprisingly large number of options. If one were to conclude that neither deadly conflicts nor avoidance or walls of separation offer sustainable solutions for urban living, the only alternative is to make an effort to engage in conversation, take the risk of interaction, and accept that people are strangers to each other. However, this only works if people trust each other. But why would the other, who has strange convictions, be trustworthy? Trust is difficult in societies where today's "traders of fear" in politics and media teach us that, in times of uncertainty and chaos, we should fear the others. At this point in human history, we need to decide how to cope with crucial choices that have to be made about the inevitability of "conflictual coexistence."

That people should learn how to converse in a disarming way is obviously important, so offering a menu of courses, seminars, and books on this communicative skill would be tempting—much like is done in books such as *Communicating Effectively for Dummies* (2001), in training manuals on cross-cultural communication competence, or in seminars on nonviolent communication (Rosenberg, 2003). All these efforts focus on improving communication skills. This is undoubtedly all terribly important and much needed. However, the first priority should be to create the conditions under which people will at all be inspired or seduced into the disarming conversation. Under what conditions does urban space offer an environment that is conducive to this type of interaction? A guiding consideration in dealing with this question may be that both too much communality and too much diversity make meaningful human communication difficult, if not impossible.

If urban space is too homogenized, like in the increasingly popular shopping mall, diversity tends to be negated. In the mall, we are all the same: fun shoppers having a good time. What is there to converse about? The "mallization" of the city does not provide optimal conditions for the communicative city. In addition to its Disney Park–type lifestyle homogenization, there are serious limits to the freedom of speech and little, if any, privacy in the private space of the mall. Conversely, if urban space is too differentiated, the urbanites may also have nothing to converse about. The gated communities and the Bronx districts have little to say to each other! The "fragmented city" obviously obstructs a communicative environment. It destroys the possibility to communicate about the perceptions, expectations, grievances, humiliations, or hatred that people may harbor.

The communicative conditions that are essential for preventing the escalation of urban conflict are the collective responsibility of the urbanites to develop the communicative city.

RIGHT TO THE COMMUNICATIVE CITY

The notion of the communicative city is the embodiment of a fundamental human right. It represents the entitlement to an urban environment in which architectural, spatial, psychological, topological, and time-related conditions invite people to impart, seek, receive, and exchange information, ideas, and opinions, and to listen to each other and learn from each other in an ambiance where their autonomy, security, and freedom are optimally guaranteed. Actually, the right to the communicative city brings together a whole set of other human rights, such as the right to free association, to privacy, and to participation in cultural life. In addition to the earlier concept of the right to the city that was developed by French philosopher Henri Lefebvre in his book *Le droit à la ville* (1968), the "human right to a communicative city" should be developed in modern urban spaces. The right to the city was inspired by the basic belief that decision-making processes in the cities should be reframed so that all urban dwellers have the right to participate in urban politics and the mechanisms that shape their environment. The right to the city has been explored by researchers in cities such as Rome, Paris, Toronto, and Sydney. A great deal of work has focused on access to public space, urban citizenship, marginalization, exclusion, and women's rights to the city. Communication as conversation is not among the topics of urban research. In the literature on the right to the city, however, there are references to access to public information and to the right of free expression, but not to interactive urban communication as conversation. In the World Charter on the Right to the City, the notion of interactive communication does not appear, so any revision of the charter should include the right to a communicative city.[2]

Without trying to be exhaustive, some of the conditions that create an urban space that invites disarming conversation can be provisionally listed:

- *Public Space.* Does the city—despite the processes of privatization—have enough public space left for people to meet?
- *Privatized Public Space.* Does the city have places that—although privately owned—function as public meeting places (one's favorite pub)?
- *Freedom.* Do meeting places provide for "free speech"? Can people express opinions and ideas without risking intervention by 24/7 audio/video surveillance?
- *Trust.* Can people communicate in spaces where they feel safe?[3]
- *Time.* Are there time constraints on access to public meeting places—such as closing hours of public parks—that may restrict opportunities for social interaction?
- *Comfort.* Are the places where people can sit and rest, like benches in parks, sufficiently comfortable?
- *Outdoor Activities.* Are there small markets and easily accessible cultural events?

- *Flexibility.* Does the city have a good balance between large, open spaces and small, intimate spaces?
- *Diversity.* Is there a variety of architectural structures and socio-economic functions, like in the world's great street?
- *Noise Levels.* Does the city have a balanced range of sound volumes?
- *Human Scale.* Do city dwellers feel that their urban space has human proportions?
- *Playgrounds.* Are there enough playgrounds for kids, or "jeu de boules," places for adults?
- *Sites of Wonder.* Does the city offer views that inspire people to converse with others?
- *Openness.* Do city officials (like in public transportation or administration) demonstrate an openness to urban conversation?
- *Reflexivity.* Are there places (like churches and chapels) where people can withdraw for an inner conversation with themselves?

The way cities structure and manage their public space is obviously essential to any effort to enhance social interaction among urbanites. In addition to managing the physical environment, there are also economic and sociocultural elements that enhance or obstruct urban social interaction.

If we have an optimal urban grid, would urban dwellers be able to engage in disarming conversation? Beyond the physical and socioeconomic environment, there has to be a psychological environment that overcomes essential obstacles to urban conversation. This environment would have to adequately address the issues of heterogeneity, speed, and mindlessness.

HETEROGENEITY

The city is a place of heterogeneity, a place of differences. Dealing with the permanent provocation (Foucault, 2003) that heterogeneity poses is exceedingly difficult for many people. Coping with heterogeneity in communication requires that people begin recognizing the polyphonic structures of their own minds. The dialogue between different people is only possible if the internal "self" extends into the external "others." This implies that we understand our inner self as a society (Minsky, 1985) that is populated by many different "I" positions that are able to conduct dialogues among themselves.

Dialogical self-theory (Hermans, Kempen, & van Loon, 1992) proposes that the self is extended to include both internal and external positions: both I positions and positions of others. The extended self breaks through the separation between self and society. Only when we learn to communicate with the plurality of our own identities can we then communicate with others. We need to first engage in the dialogue with ourselves, that is, with all the different I positions with which we live, and then discover that others (my friend, my wife, my enemy) are part of these positions. Meaningful communication with others demands that the dialogical self is extended to these others. Only in this way can the Cartesian obstacle of the distinction between me and the other be resolved and can we communicate as members of the same universe.[4]

SPEED

The city is characterized by the tremendous speed of its movements and interactions. Disarming conversations demand time. For most city dwellers, this means that they have to learn the art of slowing down.

One of the tools the city offers its citizens are pedestrian traffic lights. In many of the world's cities, one can observe how masses of people rapidly cross streets, ignoring traffic lights unless there is a police officer nearby or if there is immediate danger of being hit by a car. However, waiting for the red traffic light is an important exercise in slowing down, and it creates the opportunity to say something to another human being. The essential problem with speed is that, whereas our bodies may move with cyberspeed, our minds are still in earlier ages. As Cosmides and Tooby have stated, "Our modern skulls house a stone age mind" (Cosmides and Tooby, 1997, p. 6). This raises the question of whether our minds can catch up with our bodies. Can our minds cope with the problems of modern urban life?

This is a particularly challenging question in view of the observation that humans prefer natural environments to human-made environments. The so-called "savanna hypothesis" (Orians, 1980 and 1986) suggests that "humans seem to prefer savanna-like environments that offer prospect (resources) and refuge (places to hide)" (Buss, 2009, p. 91). If, indeed, the savanna (where humans most likely originated) is our natural habitat, living in modern urban settings is bound to be very stressful and, thus, potentially explosive.

MINDLESSNESS

Much of urban interaction is mindless. People run without seeing faces, pass others as strangers in the night, without feelings of responsibility toward others. People speed along the urban routes in psychological cocoons that broadcast the signal that "I don't mind you, please don't mind me!" Thus, the mindlessness of modern urban life produces the mindless mode of speech that was discussed in the previous chapter.

It is more characteristic of urban than of village life that numerous bystanders see a fellow human being beaten and kicked and don't intervene. They may even complain if other onlookers stand in their line of sight. Modern cities need massive training programs in mindfulness, and this is particularly urgent because cities—as will be discussed in the following chapter—are, throughout history, places of risky conflicts.

An important question that inevitably comes up is whether mindful communication and the communicative city are unrealistic propositions. Most contemporary thinking about the communicative behavior of city people has been influenced by a classical article on urban sociology by Louis Wirth titled "Urbanism as a Way of Life." According to Wirth (1938), the city is characterized by the size of its population, density of life, and heterogeneity. As a result, urbanites develop a modality of coexistence that is impersonal, fleeting, and one-dimensional (p. 12). Most contacts in the city have a businesslike, flat character.

Critics of Wirth's observation have pointed out that cities are more complex and multilayered and consist of many different domains and spaces in which people relate to each other in a variety of ways. The communicative city, then, is inspired by those urban sociologists, like Thaddeus Müller, whose work demonstrates that urban social life in the public domain can be "warm." Interactions among people in the city's public space can be personal and intimate and not necessarily anonymous and cold (Müller, 2002). Müller's findings—based on his research in Amsterdam—indicate that "urbanites make the public realm meaningful by wilfully and playfully interacting with others in this realm" (p. 189)[5]

CONCLUSION

If cities do become the collective future of humankind, we urgently need to find creative approaches to the management of urban conflicts. One such possible approach is the development of urban space in ways that facilitate "disarming conversation." This kind of urban interaction recognizes the reality of urban conflict and offers a tool to prevent conflicts from escalating from safety zones into danger zones. This is particularly important because cities are key venues for dangerous collective conflicts in the foreseeable future. Such and related collective conflicts are discussed in chapter 6.

CHAPTER **6**

COLLECTIVE EVIL
CAN IT HAPPEN AGAIN?

⊷

"For all the centuries of experience, men have not yet learned how to live together without compounding their vices and covering each other 'with mud and blood.'"

Reinhold Niebuhr (1932)

COLLECTIVE CONFLICT AND EVIL-DOING

The collective dimension of evil—in both its physical and psychological manifestations—is particularly important in this book. The most devastating conflicts occur between groups or against groups. Throughout history, groups have been killed en masse: the Philistines by the Israelites; the Carthaginians by the Romans; the "pagans" by the Crusaders; the Huguenots by Louis XIV; the indigenous people of Latin America by the Spanish conquistadors; the Armenians by the Turks; the Jews by the Nazis; the inhabitants of Hiroshima and Nagasaki by American nuclear bombs; the numerous citizens of Dresden by British firebombing; the political dissidents by Stalin (30 million), Mao (20 million), and Pol Pot (2.5 million); and some 800,000 Rwandan Tutsi by Rwandan Hutus.

Furthermore, there are devastating and gruesome contemporary illustrations of intergroup conflict in India, Sri Lanka, the Congo, Côte d'Ivoire, Rwanda, Iraq, Afghanistan, and Darfur. The twentieth century witnessed the greatest number of systematic slaughters of human beings of any century in history (Power, 2002; see also Tuchman, 1979). Indeed, this century may become historically infamous for introducing the sinister type of aggression that is called genocide. Coined by Rafael Lemkin, a Polish Jew who escaped the Holocaust and lobbied tirelessly for the international legal recognition of the mass killing of groups of people as crimes against humanity, the term did not exist in the homicide lexicon until after World War II. The UN Convention on the Prevention and Punishment of the Crime of Genocide (1948a) recognized all acts committed with the intent to destroy, in whole or in part, a national, ethnical, racial, or religious group as crimes. These crimes include killing members of a group, causing serious bodily harm or mental harm to members of a group, deliberately inflicting on the group conditions of life to bring about its destruction in whole or in part, imposing measures intended to prevent births within a group, and forcibly transferring children of a group to another group (Power, 2002).

In wars, members of groups are killed by members of other groups. The assassins are often uniformed military, security, or police personnel. But people serving in these forces (those who are "licensed to kill") are, at the end of the day, just ordinary people. Most wars and armed conflicts are, in fact, lethal confrontations between ordinary people. Ordinary people—and not their political or religious leaders—kill themselves as suicide bombers. Ordinary young people kill other ordinary young people in Afghanistan, Iran, Peru, or Zimbabwe. Their leaders are rarely if ever seen waving machetes or carrying AK-47 automatic rifles. Ordinary Americans tortured and humiliated ordinary Iraqis in Abu Ghraib. The "capos" who inspired and sanctioned this violence stayed home. Since 1945 somewhere between 18 and 25 million civilians have been murdered in different wars. What's more, this count does not include the number of civilians who were tortured, raped, illegally detained, forcefully displaced, or severely traumatized. And even then, we only count the direct victims of violence. All these millions had loved ones, families, friends, and colleagues who were left with unspeakable bereavement. In a variety of atrocious violent acts associated with intergroup conflict, around 180 million people were killed in the twentieth century. Estimates of casualties during World War

II alone are between 50 and 70 million (Rummel, 1997). Most of this violence can be seen as the collective destruction of human dignity.

The most perplexing questions in group massacres are: Why do ordinary people destroy their fellow humans? How do they become involved with evil deeds against others? Why do they collectively destroy human dignity? To explore these questions, we need look at differences between individual and collective behavior.

There is a deep distinction between the social behavior of individuals and social groups. As Rienhold Niebuhr (1932) has convincingly argued, the morals of individuals do not guide the morals of the group. Individuals are able to achieve levels of consideration, empathy, and altruism that groups cannot. Approaches to conflict de-escalation that are based on educational insights and that see ignorance as a basic source of conflict will not work on groups that are steered primarily by the collective self-interest. Collective egoism drives groups in their conflicts with other groups to unimaginable levels of cruelty. Groups are not capable of empathizing with the interests of other groups. Niebuhr (1932) suggested that there is a rift between individual and social morality, stating,

> An individual may sacrifice his own interests, either without hope of reward or in the hope of an ultimate compensation. But how is an individual, who is responsible for the interests of his group, to justify the sacrifice of interests other than his own? (p. 267)

Thus, people can be altruistic with their own interests, but being altruistic with the interests of others is unacceptable. The actions of groups are bound to be driven by collective egoism. If groups hope to achieve their selfish aims, they will fail if they apply the rules of individual morality. If oppressed minorities approach their oppressors with understanding, empathy, and consideration, they will be exploited even more. To liberate themselves, they must take forceful action against their opponents. Niebuhr (1932, p. 272) also noted that "The selfishness of human communities must be regarded as an inevitability" and that "The moral obtuseness of human collectives makes a morality of disinterestedness impossible." Thus, although there may be sentiments of commonness and individuals may recognize similarities that can mitigate the social conflict, they cannot make the conflict go away. Politics as a collective effort is always on a collision course with principles of individual morality, and as such, it may be possible to settle conflicts among individuals through reasoning, persuasion, and compromise: "In inter-group relations this is practically an impossibility" (Gilkey, 2001, p. xxxi).

Although groups are obviously composed of individuals, each with their personal psychological characteristics, the collective behavior of large groups manifests its own specific psychological dynamics.

First of all, all individuals in societies relate to some degree to groups that are essential in developing their individual identity, their existential meaning, and their future perspectives. Groups give answers to such questions as "where do I come from," "who am I and what is the sense of being me," and "where do I go, what is my destiny." However, the collective answers to such questions render people vulnerable to the manipulation of their collective identity. As group cohesion grows, the individual members of the group will tend to ask fewer critical questions and identify more with the suggested collective identity. The more cohesive in-groups become, the greater the external disconnectedness from out-groups. As the us-versus-them dichotomy grows stronger, the intergroup conflict tends to escalate more quickly. The self-respect of the group members is "tied to believing that their own group is better than other groups" (Pruitt & Kim, 2004, p. 133). As increasingly intense feelings of responsibility for other members of the in-group combine with the anonymity of crowds, which diffuses individual responsibility toward members of the out-group, this becomes a lethal mixture. Blaming, dehumanizing, and, ultimately, killing members of the out-group becomes easier, and this is particularly so when the conflict involves groups with different religions and cultures.

Secondly, individuals in groups develop a strong dependence on social approval and, as a result, concede to social pressures. An illustration of this is the Japanese kamikaze pilots during World War II. We now know that many of them preferred not to kill themselves but found it shameful to disobey orders.

Thirdly, it is difficult to establish clear accountability for collective acts as they tend to be performed in relative anonymity. As Dave Grossman concluded, "groups can provide a diffusion of responsibility that will enable individuals in mobs and soldiers in military units to commit acts that they would never dream of doing as individuals" (1995, p. 152). Killing that serves no immediate human needs—like in the overkill found in collective aggression—is more characteristic of group behavior than of individual conduct.

Lastly—and most important in group dynamics—is that collective violence is difficult to stop. Once it begins, it becomes a mission. By the time mass killing and collective humiliation are set in motion, it becomes very difficult to stop the collective violence. Destructive behavior changes the world vision and the value system of those who participate in it. What people in other times might have seen as impossible, inhuman, and atrocious now becomes the normal and right thing to do. Within the in-group, "groupthink" plays a crucial role, and this discourages members of the group from asking questions, raising objections, or dissenting. Collective destruction of human dignity becomes like a perpetual mobile and it is difficult—if not impossible—to stop it without forms of external intervention. At some point in the process, the conflict is so contagious that it keeps spreading, attracts new actors, and widens its area of impact (Schattschneider, 1960).

Nonetheless, groups also have positive potential and can achieve collectively impressive goals. Thus, although groups may not be inherently inclined to evil, there is evidence in social psychology to conclude that "the average of group members' opinions and behaviors becomes more extreme as a result of group interaction" (Waller, 2007, p. 39), which makes groups more dangerous than their individual members. James Waller (2007, p. 40) proposed that "it is the nature of the individuals that make up the collective." The collective is composed of different individuals, some who are more inclined to good and some who are more inclined to evil, and these individuals each have a genius for both good and evil (Fromm, 1964, p. 123). This is a delicate balance that is easily disturbed toward evil under the conditions of the spiral of escalation (as elaborated in chapter 2). If and when this happens, the dynamics of collective behavior render halting or reversing the course of destructive action extremely difficult.

The most confrontational questions we face are: Could it happen again? Could people kill and humiliate each other once again in such great numbers? Could this happen only in "anocracies"—unstable regimes in transition to democracies? Or, could it also happen in established democracies? The path to finding an answer leads us first of all to question just how risky and insecure today's world really is.

THE PRESENT STATE OF GROUP CONFLICT IN THE WORLD

There are potential crisis situations in the current international system that are risks for security. Such crises facilitate the escalation of hostile interactions toward serious armed confrontation.

Trends in armed conflicts in the world from 1945 to 2005 (Hewitt, Wilkenfeld, & Gurr, 2008) show that since the 1960s, most violent conflicts are internal. The substantial increase in the amount of internal warfare in 2005 brought the global total of active conflicts to twenty-five, the highest total since 2001. Even more sobering is that the increase from the 2004 total of nineteen represents the single largest annual increase in global conflict since 1990. A closer look at what happened in 2005 reveals that many of the "new" conflicts in that year were actually renewed hostility in long-standing conflicts that had temporarily subsided.

Although the frequency of explosive crises has declined since the end of the Cold War, those that do occur are more prone than earlier crises to escalating violence. This means that a much smaller proportion of conflicts escapes the escalation dynamic whereby violence begets violence. One reason for the danger of remaining crisis situations is that their escalation may involve nuclear violence. The 2008 Peace and Conflict study (Hewitt et al., 2008) reported in earlier editions evidence of a decline in armed conflicts within states in the early twenty-first century. The most recent report (Hewitt et al., 2010), however, points to new developments that undermine human security. Although the average death tolls of armed conflicts may have decreased, "A larger portion of the global community of states is involved now than in any other time in the past six decades" (Hewitt et al., 2010, p. 1).

In 2010 there were five protracted conflicts in the world that can easily escalate: between India and Pakistan, Israel and Palestine, Taiwan and China, North and South Korea, and Iraq and Iran. In 2008 there were at least six countries where the risk of genocidal and political violence was very high: Sudan (target groups: Darfuri, Southerns, Nuba), Myanmar (target groups: Karen and other separatists), Pakistan (target groups: Ahmadis, Shi'I), Bhutan (target group: Lhotshampas), Iran (target groups: Kurds, Baha'is), and Syria (target group: Kurds).[1]

Armed conflicts are often about self-determination. In late 2006, twenty-six armed conflicts of self-determination were ongoing. Among them were conflicts in India, Myanmar, Ethiopia, the Middle East, and Russia. Groups involved in self-determination conflicts use militant tactics (mass protest, boycotts, strikes), engage in different levels of hostilities (armed assault, bombing), or even engage in serious warfare. Hewitt et al. (2008) noted that

It is true that independence-minded groups are more likely to fight wars than groups with other objectives. The protagonists of the six most deadly wars were the Chechens in Russia, Kashmiris in India, Kurds in Turkey, Tamils in Sri Lanka and Karens and Shans in Burma. (p. 5)

However, not all self-determination movements rely on violent tactics. Many of these groups currently support significant movements using conventional political means in their pursuit of self-determination goals. Movements such as the Wallons (in Belgium), or the Jurassians (in Switzerland) use such political institutions.

The urgent danger spots in the early twenty-first century are Afghanistan (the explosive combination of a guerrilla war, clashing tribal identities, religious motives, and external intervention), Iraq (local political and religious battles, guerilla warfare, foreign occupation, control over oil reserves), Ethiopia (with self-determination liberation fronts against the central government), India (with the Indian/Pakistani territorial conflict and religiously inspired confrontations), Myanmar (self-determination conflicts and confrontations between the military administration and the prodemocracy movement), and Sri Lanka, Sudan, Uganda, and the Congo (Hewitt et al., 2008, p. 12).

Since the 1950s, seventy-nine territorially concentrated ethnic groups have waged armed conflicts for autonomy or independence. Although no new conflicts have erupted since 2005, two previously contained self-determination movements experienced renewed hostilities in recent years: the Kurds in Iran and the South Ossetians in Georgia. The Iranian Kurds had pursued conventional politics for almost nine years before a mid-2005 series of violent demonstrations quickly moved from a set of isolated incidents to more frequent low-level clashes with the government (Hewitt et al., 2008, p. 37). The 2008 Peace and Conflict report warns that

The average lethality of war has declined for those caught up in combat, but not for civilians in guerrilla wars. Of 81 states that fought large-scale insurgencies from 1945–2000, one in three resorted to mass killing of civilians that are thought to support the rebels. The greater the civilian support for guerrillas and the greater the guerillas' threat to the government, the more likely governments are to choose a deliberate policy of mass killing. (Hewitt et al., 2008, p. 2)

A deeply worrisome trend in current conflicts is that religious motivations are increasingly incorporated in ethno-politics and that religion as political ideology is continually rising. This is dangerous because the enemy who is disrespectful of what is held to be most valuable is seen as the dehumanized devil that needs to be destroyed.

Religious beliefs represent the sacredness of important values, and it is the mission of the chosen people to defend these beliefs. The non-believers deserve to be discriminated against and eventually eliminated. In combination with apocalyptic interpretations, deploying all means of destruction is easily justified.

In today's societies, people cannot escape the confrontation with others who find their deepest convictions totally abject and even dangerous. They will inevitably be profoundly hurt. Rejecting an individual's essential beliefs touches on issues of human dignity because it takes an important part of human existence away. This cannot be conveniently argued away by reference to the democratic necessity to tolerate criticism. At the same time, we cannot deny those who offend others the right to express their existential fear of the stranger and his strange convictions. This would not only violate the constitutional right to freedom of speech, but, more importantly, it would violate the fundamental and absolute human right to freedom of thought.

All the major religions have experienced religiously inspired violence, which tends to be unlimited. Any act undertaken in the name of God is, by definition, justified, however gruesome it may be. Innocent bystanders may be killed, but in the end, God, for whom the destruction is wrought, will pardon the perpetrators. Because of this, the destruction is deeply meaningful to its perpetrators and to many of their supportive audiences. In this way, religious violence does make sense: It also gives purpose to otherwise insignificant lives. The rational calculation that the violence may not lead to immediate victory and may indeed be very costly is hardly convincing to the true believer. In the end, the struggle will be won. And in the short run, there are rewards in heaven or paradise. And, in any case, martyrdom is a highly sought social status. Furthermore, the destruction caused by the protagonists of the good is seen as insignificant compared to the damage wrought by the representatives of evil. These followers of Satan—demons—need to be killed before they get a chance to kill the forces of good. Therefore, because in religious conflict the deepest truths are at stake, compromise is not easily possible, and it may even be seen as impossible. One does not make deals with Satan.

Religious movements that preach their belief as the ultimate truth are, by definition, intolerant. Their more extremist members (such as Sikh extremists or Hindu nationalists) pose a great escalation risk, as they feel that letting others get away as nonbelievers amounts to the betrayal of God. They are ready to pursue their intolerance through violent means. Some even see violent acts as their religious duty (the Islamic Jihad in Egypt). Religious conflict is often seen by extremists as the manifestation on earth of the cosmic struggle between the forces of good and evil, between God and Satan.

In the confrontation with Islamist movements, Western governments tend to use military and propagandist techniques that confirm the existence of a war of cosmic proportions. This draws those governments and their citizens into wars such as in Afghanistan and Iraq.

The discussion about whether religions are in themselves conflict oriented and prone to the use of violence is not very meaningful. Such discussions about generalities like the essence of human beings tend to be very unproductive and inconclusive. What does matter, however, is that the (perceived) religious identity can be manipulated for destructive action. If leaders can make their followers believe that the core of their identity (their faith) is threatened, bloody revenge against the other faith can easily follow.

The most striking feature of today's bloody conflicts is the rate of recurrence. Out of the twenty-six active armed conflicts at the beginning of 2008, most were renewed fighting after hostilities had subsided briefly. Hewitt et al. (2010, p. 27) observed that "The return of significant violence in Peru is an example of the growing problem of conflict recurrence." The phenomenon of "conflict recurrence" was already mentioned in chapter 1.

THE THREE ESSENTIAL CONFLICTS TODAY

The current state of violent conflicts in the world makes the planet a dangerous place. The increasingly explosive urbanization of the world, the situations in which groups entertain inimical claims that relate to the access to essential resources, and clashes over differences of identity all further intensify this danger.

Urban-Based Conflicts

"Cities are the collective future of humankind."

Kofi Annan

Most conflict literature focuses on individuals, groups, and states, whereas little attention is given to the urban dimension of human life and its role in conflict situations. This is odd, as cities are increasingly important actors in matters of war and peace.

As discussed in chapter 5, in the twenty-first century, the human species will, for the first time in history, become an "urban species." In 2009 half of the global population lived in urban areas and in the years to come it was expected to reach some 70%. The city will be the space in which people have to find ways to live together and to deal with all the conflicts that accompany urban spaces.

For example, Latin America is the most urbanized region in the developing world, with 77% of its population—433 million people—living in cities. What's more, Latin America's urbanization has yet to reach its peak. By 2015 the UN predicts that 81% of its population will reside in urban areas. Similarly, Asia and Africa face very intense urbanization. Asia alone will account for more than half the world's urban population by 2030, and in that same year the African urban population will be larger than the total population of Europe.

The world has never before known so many and such large cities, as the massive conurbations of more than 20 million people are now gaining ground in Asia, Latin America, and Africa. Many of these cities have populations larger than entire countries. The population of Greater Mumbai (which will soon achieve megacity status), for instance, is already larger than the total population of Norway and Sweden combined. As these cities increase and grow, the quality and sustainability of life in the world's cities will largely depend on the ways in which the urbanites manage to coexist with each other.

* * *

As long as there have been cities, there has been urban conflict. Early signs come from one of the world's oldest cities, Tell Brak in Syria, where in 2006 prehistoric mass graves were discovered. According to archaeologists, the unearthed remains were victims of a bloody urban massacre that took place almost 6,000 years ago. The lead researcher, Jason Ur from Harvard University, commented that

> Given Brak's status as one of the earliest cities in the Near East … it is not impossible that this violence was the result of growing pains— internal social conflict brought about by the processes of urbanization, an entirely new phenomenon at this early date. (quoted in J. Owen, 2007, September 7)

In the late Middle Ages, the cities of the Low Countries (among them Bruges and Ghent) that had grown rapidly became stages of great economic and political conflict. These conflicts found expression in the ways parties managed urban space to meet their partisan interests. New urban power holders, such as artisans and their guilds, developed impressive manifestations of their authority through buildings such as town halls and guild houses. Conflicts arose on such issues as the fiscal claims made by the governing princes and dukes against the claims of the urban artisans. However, the battles between nobility and artisans were not simply about economic issues; they also involved political power (Boone, 2002). Many medieval towns have histories of discriminatory measures against immigrants from rural areas who became urban outcasts, or against minorities such as the Jews in Rome and Avignon who were confined to live in ghettos with severe constraints on their economic and social activities. Furthermore, in fourteenth-century multicultural London, there were violent riots against foreigners and, then in the fifteenth century, many violent outbursts of xenophobia.

Urban violence seems to be a permanent feature of human history. In November of 2006, two gangs in the slum valley of Mathare (Nairobi, Kenya) fought violently over the issue of control over the illegal brewing market in the slum. Eight people died and some 9,000 were displaced. These kinds of events are increasingly not exceptional. According to the UN-Habitat Report "Enhancing Safety and Security—Global Report on Human Settlements 2007," urban violence and crime is on the rise. As the report states, "Over the past five years, 60 per cent of all urban residents in developing countries have been victims of crime" (UN-Habitat, 2007). At the request of African mayors, UN-Habitat launched in 1996 its Safer Cities programs to develop city-level crime-prevention strategies.

The inherently conflictual nature of urban space is the result of several forces that reinforce each other. First, cities confront their inhabitants with clearly visible disparities between the affluent and the impoverished. In particular, cities in developing countries show enormously vast and very visible gaps between the rich and the poor. Most cities have a (globally networked) urban elite and an urban mass. It is not uncommon that the elite benefits from the disadvantaged position of the masses. For example, the marginalized masses can be exploited for their cheap labor. Furthermore, the fear of crime among the better-off reinforces segregation, as the rich protect themselves by building gated communities, which causes further socioeconomic exclusion and stigmatization for the urban poor. The resulting fragmentation of the city continues to create even more moments of violent and criminal conduct. Segregated spatial arrangements that are intended to enforce security can themselves become sources of high-security risks.

Second, cities have always been places where people emigrated from impoverished rural areas or from war-torn regions. City administrations have always had to deal with "alien politics." They had to address questions about which foreigners to welcome (usually the more prosperous), which ones to deport (usually the poor), and which ones to grant local welfare services or even citizenship. The waves of migration throughout history—dating from antiquity, the middles ages, the reformation, and the counter-reformation, through an eighteenth-century cosmopolitan Enlightenment to twentieth-century mass-labor and industrial migration—have always primarily affected the cities.

Third, most cities face the problem of rapidly expanding populations while the provisions of adequate infrastructures and services lags behind. Most big cities in developing countries have a rapidly growing "illegal city," which is characterized by poor living conditions, overcrowded houses, unemployment, lack of clean water, poor sanitation, and violent crime.

Fourth, cities are more competitive and more differentiated than rural areas, and the heterogeneity of urban populations is much larger than among rural populations.

Fifth, the city is also the place of frustration. Those who migrate to the city dream of limitless opportunities that, in reality, urban life does not offer. Life in the city does not provide all city dwellers with economic improvement. Even though cities are places of economic growth, employment opportunities, and cultural creativity, they are also sites of poor shelter, unemployment, bad sanitation, air pollution, and overcrowded public transportation (UN-Habitat, 2006, p. 10).

Sixth, evidence shows that the probability of being a victim of crime and violence is substantially higher in urban areas than in rural areas.

Seventh, cities are crowded spaces that offer easy and soft targets for terrorist and insurgency groups. In an increasingly urbanized world, such groups, rather than seeking shelter within rural groups, are colonizing the world's burgeoning urban spaces (Graham, 2006, p. 151). Recent events in New York; Washington, D.C.; Madrid; London; Nairobi; and Dar es Salaam are all telling illustrations.

Finally, an inherent tension and oversensitivity exists in movements of large numbers of people who are unknown to each other, insecure about the potential threats others pose, and interact anonymously but often very closely, almost intimately. The urban space where strangers interact with strangers easily breeds "street rage." The city is full of explosive places—an insignificant car collision may operate like lighting a cigarette in an ammunition depot.

* * *

Cities are the key hubs in global economic activity and key actors in current processes of globalization. The January 17, 2008 issue of *Time* magazine featured a cover story detailing how three connected cities (New York, London, and Hong Kong, aptly titled Nylonkong) drive the global economy (Elliott, 2008, January 17). Their shared economic energy creates a powerful network that both illustrates and explains globalization. They are not only centers of money exchange and high finance, but they are also centers of culture! Cultural production and consumption has become an important element of the economies of the world's big cities and this has introduced new ways to use urban space for public cultural performances, where a variety of cultural roles merge, such as those of spectatorship, tourism, performance, and sales. The big cities have also become key places for all kinds of services, such as legal assistance, marketing, advertising and architecture (Sassen, 2001).

In the next section, we will look at the major types of urban conflicts.

Urban Warfare

According to the Worldwatch Institute,[2] urban unrest is likely to increase in the largest cities of the developing world as more and more people from diverse ethnic and religious groups increasingly come into close contact with each other. Although cities offer the opportunity for diverse interests to integrate, when resources are scarce or when political interests collide, they can also become sites of warfare. Cities such as Los Angeles, Belfast, Sarajevo, and Mogadishu have all suffered from some form of urban warfare.

High levels of urban crime and violence affect the social fabric of entire cities. They cause urban residents to feel fear and suspicion, which often leads the wealthy to fortify their residences, building higher walls around their homes and spending more on private security—in effect "locking themselves" in enclaves that are physically separated from the rest of the city (UN-Habitat, 2007, p. 145). In many big cities, people's fear of crime leads them to abandon and stigmatize certain neighbor-hoods and develop an "architecture of fear" (UN-Habitat, 2006, p. 145). Urban insecurity creates fragmented cities with securely protected "gated communities" and "no-go areas." This insecurity threatens cities' ability to socially and economically develop because it hampers urban mobility and cohesion, thus "undermining the interchange, openness, flow and density that sustain cities in the first place" (Graham, 2006, p. 151).

Security

Security has always been a prime feature of city development. Their economic importance made cities prime targets for warfare and political struggle. Today's big cities seem obsessed with security, thus develop-ing ever wider and more intrusive forms of surveillance over citizens. Davis observed that "The universal consequence of the crusade to secure the city is the destruction of any truly democratic urban space" (Davis, 1992, p. 155). The proliferation of security measures—such as street surveillance, control of public areas, and the curtailment of civil liberties like the freedom of association or expression—threatens the core of urban life.

Evidence shows that a person is more likely to be a victim of crime and violence in urban areas than in rural areas.[3] Consequently, urban insecurity presents a major challenge to the social and economic de-velopment of cities because it also compounds other factors, such as poverty and social exclusion, which already limit the quality of life for many. Insecurity further contributes to the isolation of groups and to the stigmatization of certain neighborhoods, particularly those in which the poor and more vulnerable live. It creates conditions of fear, hinders mobility, and may be a major stumbling block for community participa-tion, social cohesion, and full citizenship.

Resources

Worldwide, as people face increasingly gross inequities in their access to scarce resources, there is a rapidly growing danger of violent conflict over natural resources. There are—certainly in the cities of poor countries—urban conflicts over access to water, quality of water (pollution of ground-water, sanitation issues), pricing and management of the distribution of water (private versus public), and access to electricity and food.

Youth

In South Asian cities, there is an explosive potential for violent conflict as the youth population grows and urban poverty deepens. Today, South Africa's big cities face a generation of young people who, even at a very early age, use violence easily and as a matter of course. The "youth bulge" is a particularly explosive ingredient, particularly in the slums, where almost 50% of the population is under 20. In the Kenyan city Nairobi, most violent crimes are committed by youths belonging to the Mungiki movement, which boasts some 2 million members.

The youth who spoke out during and after the riots in Paris in 2005 protested vehemently over two questions employers consistently asked during job interviews: the applicants' ethnic origins and their address. In addition to ethnic discrimination, employers were also known to discriminate against those who lived in stigmatized neighborhoods. Similarly, in Rio de Janeiro, a study found that living in a favela appeared to be a bigger barrier to gaining employment than being dark skinned or female (UN-Habitat, 2006, p. 123).

Religion

The mosque conflicts in European cities illustrate religion-related conflicts in the contemporary, urban age. In many European cities, such as Amsterdam, Paris, Berlin, or London, one can now find sizable Muslim immigrant communities. As a result, more and more mosques are being built, which raises concerns in many non-Islamic communities. Cesari (2005, p. 1018) has argued that "The mosque not only expresses the presence of a local Muslim community, it also represents the evolution of Islam from the private to the public sphere." By and large, then, local communities resent this transformation of the public sphere and express concerns about the Islamicization of urban, public space.

Ethnicity

Around the world, ethnic groups are in conflict with other ethnic groups about real or perceived forms of discrimination, denials of their identities, disrespect for their otherness, and lack of social and economic opportunities. In particular, ethnic-communal conflicts are widespread in Third World cities, such as Karachi and Ahmedabad. Nonetheless, urban ethnic diversity is an essential element of urban life and the global city (Sassen, 2001), reinforcing both ethnic differences and ethnic segregation.

Segregation

In many cities, one finds safe pedestrian quarters, with lavish fountains and piazzas and comfortable benches, whereas a short distance away, one can also find areas where poverty reigns. In these latter areas, the city administration does little to keep streets liveable. As a result, the world has close to 1 billion slum dwellers who live in the city but are excluded from the key urban infrastructures and services. The vast majority of slums—more than 90%—are located in cities of the developing world.

The "dual" city reflects the broader asymmetrical world order that is characterized by division and exclusion. In many cities, one finds the two parallel processes, commonly known as Disneyfication (the city as "theme park," Sorkin, 1992) and Bronxification (the city as place of violence and crime). In the Disneyfied urban space, conflict is denied. There is no trouble in Disneyland, where everything is predictable and controlled (Wasko, 2001). The "reality" of Disneyland is one-dimensional, and thus the city has to be regularly cleansed of unwanted persons. The poor sometimes intrude on the city center, so city administrators design plans to deport the "deviants" to places where they cannot be seen by decent city dwellers. When the unwanted persons try to survive on the streets, many city governments engage in a kind of civil war against them. Conversely, in the Bronxified urban space, conflict easily escalates toward lethal violence. Here, just like in the world arena, poor people are the likely victims of other poor people perpetrating acts of violence.

Environment

Here, urban conflict focuses on clashes between environmentalists, labor, business, and city administrators over issues of economic growth versus ecological safety. The tendency to develop cities at the expense of the natural environment is increasingly challenged by the recent excitement about planning "green cities," and thus different visions of city management and its spatial planning collide.

Anticitizen Conflict

As part of the global "war on terror," many city administrations define their own citizens as enemies and want to control them through military means (Graham, 2004, p. 227). Recent large investments in anticitizen weapons are just one illustration of this phenomenon. However, such measures against terrorism seriously endanger the conviviality in cities. As Madeleine Bunting commented, "Cities have become our battlegrounds" (quoted in Graham, 2004, p. 334). And Robert Warren analyzed,

> The militarization of urban spaces in North America and Europe in other-than-war conditions is a frequent and expanding occurrence and affects governance on two scales. It undermines both democratic control over a city by its residents, and the critical ability of localities to provide the public space in which citizens can mobilize to express political voice on global issues when no democratic institutional means are available. (2004, p. 229)

The danger of the city's militarization is that "fortress cities" emerge, which obstruct the development of urban communicative environments. As a result, urban conflict becomes more aggravated, as the possibility to communicate about the grievances, humiliations, and hatred that people may harbor is destroyed.

Resource-Based Conflicts

Throughout history, there have been disputes—which often escalated into full wars—over the access to and control over basic resources such as land and water. At the beginning of the twenty-first century, resources continue to be major sources of conflicts that could easily escalate. Today, the most threatened resources are oil and water. The demands for oil and water are rapidly increasing as more people and increasing numbers of prosperous people demand more of them. With the world population expected to grow to some 9 billion by 2050, industrial, agricultural, and consumer demands for oil and water will also double by that same year. There are no indications this will slow, and where the supplies will come from is unclear. Scarcity of energy and water resources will inevitably lead to food shortages that can possibly be resolved through diplomatic negotiations about redistribution and through political and trade agreements to cooperate, but with decreases in agricultural production and diminishing supplies of fresh water in combination with ever-growing populations, the pressures on governments to use violence will likewise grow, which means resource conflicts may become resource wars.

For many countries, resource issues have become a matter of vital national security, which implies that many nations are prepared to deploy armed forces to protect their supplies of resources. Because almost all countries are dependent on energy, government policies to secure future energy supplies can easily create tensions, with the potential to escalate into energy wars. Even if the depletion of energy resources would not be a major concern, their highly unequal distribution across the world (some 30% of the world population has no electricity) provides explosive potential for the escalation of conflicts. A 2003 Pentagon report (Schwartz & Randall) on abrupt climate change develops the following scenario: "Military confrontation may be triggered by a desperate need for natural resources such as energy, food and water rather than by conflicts over ideology, religion, or national honor."[4]

Oil Conflicts

The energy community seems to generally agree on the advent of the "oil peak," which could be reached around 2020 according to estimates from the International Energy Agency. The 2008 report by the International Energy Agency (IEA) presented in London on November 12, 2008, predicts that world energy demands will expand by 45% until 2030. The IEA foresees demand for oil growing from 85 million barrels per day (the demand in 2007) to 106 million barrels per day in 2030—and the oil producers are unlikely to be able to keep up with this growth. One reason for this is that current oil fields will decline faster than was previously thought. The IEA report concludes that current energy trends are socially, economically, and environmentally unsustainable.

Oil conflicts are already present, and the dangerous mix of the rising demand for petroleum with political turmoil, ethnic divisions, the emergence of fundamentalist separatist movements, and foreign interventions can easily escalate into warfare (Klare, 2001, p. 46). Michael T. Klare (2001, p. 51) noted that "Of all the world's major oil-producing areas, the Persian Gulf region is the one most likely to experience conflict in the next century." Furthermore, in the Caucasus, oil conflicts remain frozen but could flare up anytime (Klare, 2001, p. 253, n86). In fact, the oil conflict in this region could develop into a new U.S./Russia confrontation: "With arms pouring into the area and the major powers jockeying for advantage, the Caspian basin appears headed for a recurring cycle of crisis and conflict" (Klare, 2001, p. 82).

Diminishing oil revenues could have important social effects on oil-producing countries. Oil-exporting countries in the Middle East, Latin America, and Africa have rapidly growing populations, and unless they diversify their economies, once the oil peak passes, they may confront high rates of unemployment. Howard observed, "Desperate to secure their future, these exporting countries, or factions within them, could perhaps try to stake their claim over disputed oil-rich regions or even blatantly disregard international law by attacking vulnerable neighbors" (2009, p. 19). Stealing other countries' resources, siphoning off oil from shared underground reservoirs, or exceeding agreed-upon quota are all very real options.[5]

Furthermore, in Islamist countries, there may also be the risk of violent nationalist reactions to the involvement of foreign (Western) oil companies, which are nonetheless needed because of their expertise, experience, and technology.

Water Conflicts

Another issue of conflict concerns the access to fresh water. Disputes about access to water have a long history. Water is already a contested resource in the stories of the Old Testament, and "For centuries, warfare has been associated with the protection and destruction of vital water systems" (Klare, 2001, p. 138). More recently, water conflicts erupted in the Middle East and Asia. Klare went on to state that

> Now, at the dawn of the twenty-first century, conflict over critical water supplies is an ever-present danger. In a vast area stretching from North Africa to the Near East and South Asia, the demand for water is rapidly overtaking the existing supply. (2001, p. 139)

The facts that most of the world's fresh water is not usable for human consumption and that water consumption has enormously increased in recent years are essential issues in water disputes. These disputes often concern situations in which water runs through different countries, so more countries need to share water sources. Examples include disputes between Turkey and Syria and between Syria and Iraq over the Tigris and the Euphrates rivers. Although such disputes about shared water sources can sometimes be settled in nonviolent ways, they can also erupt into violent hostilities.

The UN Development Program reported in 1999 that by 2025, one in two Africans would face water shortages, and the report expected "violent flashpoints to erupt along the Nile, and in the Niger Volta and Zambezi deltas" (Perry, 2008, November 27, p. 34). On a global scale, since 1950 the worldwide demand for water has doubled. In North Africa and the Middle East, countries lack sufficient supplies of fresh water to satisfy the needs of their populations. The UNDP Human Development Report of 2006 addressed "the global water crisis." In its introduction, the authors of the report state that each year almost 2 million children die for want of water and sanitation (United Nations, 2006). It goes on to show that more than 1 billion people do not have access to safe water. Unsafe water is a crucial factor in perpetuating poverty around the world. Particularly in the large cities in poor countries, the slums (the "informal" cities) have only limited access to water. As the UNDP reported,

> across much of the developing world competition over water (for example between urban and rural areas when cities extend their claims to water into agricultural lands) is intensifying at an alarming rate, giving rise to intense—and sometimes violent conflict.

Although over the centuries people have more often cooperated than fought over cross-border water sources, "the potential for cross-boundary tension and conflict cannot be ignored" (United Nations, 2006, p. 32).

In *Nature* of March 19, 2009, Wendy Barnaby argued that countries do not go to war over water (Barnaby, 2009, March 19).[6] The historical facts demonstrate that in the past, most water conflicts had been resolved without warfare. Barnaby's optimistic expectation that even though water shortages could lead to violence, parties usually find peaceful solutions, may indeed be too strongly based on past experiences. That conflicts over water in the past have not escalated does not necessarily lead to the conclusion that future water-resource tensions will also not escalate into destructive action.

Around the world, one easily finds evidence of strong communal tensions when the water supply is in danger. There is competition for agricultural use of water for food supplies (70%), for industrial manufacturing (20%), and for residential use (10%). When conflicts do arise, the rural areas usually lose, and this is increasingly the case as big cities' populations continue to grow quickly—almost 100 million people each year. Brown stated, "Increasingly, the world's cities are meeting their growing needs by taking irrigation water from farmers" (2008, p. 19). Cities such as Los Angeles, San Diego, Mexico City, Cairo, Chennai (India), and Izmir (Turkey) all have been known to grab or buy water from farmers and transport it to their populations. Brown went on to claim that "Whether it is outright government expropriation, farmers outbid by cities, or cities simply drilling deeper wells than farmers can afford, the world's farmers are losing the water war" (2008, p. 19).

Thus, the combination of water shortage and growing population causes major tensions in countries around the world. Brown observed,

> Recent years have witnessed conflicts over water in scores of countries, such as the competition between cities and farmers in countries like China, India and Yemen. In other countries, the conflicts are between tribes, as in Kenya, or between villages as in India and China, or between upstream and downstream water users, as in Pakistan or China. In some countries, local water conflicts have led to violence and death, as in Kenya, Pakistan, and China. (2008, p. 21)

Resource-based conflicts are explosive. They may be caused by a real scarcity or by a perceived scarcity that is seen as a fundamental threat to collective interests, which warrants a preemptive violent strike to secure these interests for the future.

These tensions can escalate if political leaders play the identity card, use old rivalries, or present violent competition as the only option. Klare observed that

> As we move deeper into the twenty-first century, the global human community faces a momentous choice: we can either proceed down the path of intensified resource competition, which will lead to recurrent outbreaks of conflict throughout the world, or we can choose to manage global resource stockpiles in a cooperative fashion. (2001, p. 225)

Thus, the choice for cooperation seems logical and rational, but human decision making is rarely logical and rational. The Pentagon 2003 report proposed that strong states will secure their control over vital resources and, if this is so, then escalating conflict is more likely than worldwide cooperation.

Chapter 6

Identity-Based Conflicts

"Protracted conflicts over the rights and demands of ethnic and religious groups have caused more misery and loss of human life than has any other type of local, regional, and international conflict since the end of World War II."

Barbara Harff and Ted Robert Gurr (2004)

Disputes about crucial resources are often linked with identity conflicts. Such conflicts are usually referred to as ethnic conflicts. However, the notion of an "ethnic conflict" is troublesome. It is a late-1960s academic construct that relies heavily on a singularist definition of groups of people. It defines people in terms of only one of their characteristics—their ethnic background. It suggests a unique specificity that—like with the term "race"—makes little sense biologically: Genetically, human beings are more similar than they are different. Moreover, there is no such thing as a single ethnic or religious identity. People live inevitably with multiple identities and operate in several different multicultural and transcultural fields (Bourdieu, 1984). For instance, your ethnic background may be Moroccan, but you are also an immigrant, a Dutch national, a woman, a student, a Muslim, a music lover, and a sports aficionado. In other words, you always have multiple identities, and some of them may also change over time, such as through transgender operations or religious conversions.

"Ethnic" tends to have a somewhat demeaning connotation, as it often refers to non-Western groups. Their ethnicity is sometimes also held to be responsible for the hostilities between groups of different ethnic backgrounds. Doing so suggests that ethnicity is the major factor in the conflict rather than an unjust distribution of power that the colonial powers themselves organized in the first place.

Ethnic differences alone are rarely the primary cause of hostilities. Nonetheless, leaders often use ethnicity to mobilize people for hostile action against others. To claim that mainly age-old ethnic rifts caused the massacres in the Hutu-Tutsi hostilities would be misleading. In fact, there were more incendiary components, like the role of the colonial powers in distributing political and economic power. Today's identity conflicts have deep historical roots in processes such as colonial rule, in which colonial rulers often favored specific groups, thus disadvantaging others. Additionally, Harff and Gurr (2004, p. 21) noted that "Colonial rule also established hierarchies and rivalries among groups where few or none had previously existed."

"Ethnicity" provides especially those people who are hit worst by resource scarcity (often the poor) with a sense of belonging to an in-group that is different from and superior to an out-group. This makes them vulnerable to agitation against others by unscrupulous leaders. The collective motivation of group conflicts is often shaped by ethnic ideologies.

A more appropriate term for "ethnic" conflict is "identity" conflict. In an identity conflict, a perceived identity of an ethnic or a religious nature is a central variable. People rally around symbols of their common background in race, ethnicity, or religion. The emotion behind saying that "we are Catholics" (or Muslims, or Serbs) has a strong cohesive significance: It stresses commonality above differentiation and renders the protection of this "imagined collective" more important than the protection of the rights and freedoms of its individual members. Those who question—let alone criticize—the wisdom of this collective senti-ment are in danger of, at best, marginalization. At the core, identity is an imaginative construct that binds people together and distinguishes them from other people.[7] The national identity can be inclusive—a space for multi-ethnicity—and exclusive; the prerogative of the self-selected indigenous tribe is to exclude other communities.

Nationalism has a strong homogenizing tendency. It demands a strong emotional attachment to a shared belief and tends to respond strongly to perceived threats to those beliefs. Identity conflicts can also occur among members of diaspora and migrant communities as well as between different generations and the experience of their identity—for example, in relation to religious practices.

Identity conflicts facilitate mass killings more easily than conflicts over politics or economy (Licklider, 1995, p. 84). In-groups execute this massive violence against groups who are characterized by ethnic and religious features or by political preferences and are seen as a threat to the power and territorial interests of the in-group. Thus, the in-group believes that they have to be removed.

Otherness

At its core, identity is a confrontation with the difference of "other-ness" and, as such, is a potential source of conflict. We can only say who we are in distinction to others who are different from us. When confronting others who are different, this otherness may be perceived as a threat to who we are: Why are they different? Why are they not the same as us? What is wrong with us? Thus, the others pose a challenge to our self-concept, to our view of the universe, and to our values and deeply held beliefs.

Heterogeneity is difficult. In a society in which people have more homogeneous lifestyles and normative positions, key values—such as free speech—are self-understood. Conversely, in a society with a heterogeneity of value positions, such shared values become a source of conflict.

However, humankind is inevitably heterogeneous. This heterogeneity is—to borrow a term from Connolly (1991)—agonistic and a permanent provocation (Foucault, 2003). This is denied by those forces that want to lock people up into a singular identity. The ethnic and religious absolutists refuse to live with this provocation of heterogeneity, thus preferring homogeneity. The ultimate denial of heterogeneity necessarily implies collective violence, as in genocidal war.

Nonetheless, identity is impossible without "alterity." People find who they are by contrasting themselves against others. This can be a violent process if the other is seen as inferior to us. Although the others are "different," that is not, in itself, a sufficient reason for violent action because many other groups are equally or even more "different" and yet they do not become enemies. Those others who are made into enemies are the people to whom we attribute the misery of our lives: They are the source of our problems and this justifies our hatred of them. Furthermore, this mechanism of attribution can be skillfully manipulated by ruthless leaders. The intergroup conflict may be about substantial issues, like access to vital resources, but it will be exacerbated by the affective issue of blaming the other for one's own misery. The affective component—they cannot be trusted and deserve to be killed—is, in any case, a strong element in prolonging conflicts and rendering them violent and cruel.

Increase

One of the world's most critical problems is the alarming and worldwide increase of identity conflicts. With almost complete certainty, it can be predicted that several violent conflicts are still to come in the near future. The potential for such clashes is extremely high in various parts of the world. Around the world, some 10,000 distinct societies have to find ways to live together in some 200 countries. What is most troublesome in the rise of these conflicts is that they are characterized by the exercise of gross violence against civil populations. Contrary to classical warfare between armies, violence now increasingly targets civilians of the fighting parties. At the dramatic core of ethnic conflicts is the grand scale on which certain groups perpetrate crimes against humanity (further discussed in chapter 7). Over the past decades, the number of countries in which such conflicts escalated into bloody wars has considerably increased. Ethnic and religious extremism and fanaticism have expanded across the world in ways that should have been unimaginable after the horrors of the Holocaust. But as "the assertion of group identities continues to be a major factor in the politics of almost every world region," also in established democracies, identity conflicts are likely to continue to be sources of escalating violence (Harff & Gurr, 2004, p. 194).

Furthermore, many modern societies are confronted with growing diaspora communities that are permanent, are increasingly assertive about their cultural identity, and, through transport and communication technology and cash flows of over US$100 billion annually (according to estimates from the International Monetary Fund), retain strong cultural bonds with their homelands. Modern states feel ill at ease with this phenomenon, and if they are not pursuing apartheid or segregationist or assimilation policies, they try integration politics. Most modern states feel uncomfortable about the loss of the monostate—the mono-ethnic, monoreligious, monocultural and mono-ideological state. States such as the Netherlands may perceive themselves as multiculturalist, but, in fact, the myth of the monostate is not easily given up, and the cloak of multiculturalism obscures what is, in fact, cultural assimilation.

In cultural assimilation, there is space for cultural identity, but it must be within the boundaries of the dominant model. The formula is simple: The indigenous tribes have developed a normative societal framework and the newcomers are invited or coerced to integrate within it. This dominant societal model is taken for granted and is not up for public deliberation. On national, regional, and global levels integration processes are always imposed from above in situations of socioeconomic inequality. This constitutes a source of growing and violent discontent.

Religion

Religious violence is a key aspect of many identity conflicts. From various sources, it can be concluded that in the 1950–1996 period, some 40% of all conflicts were religious conflicts. In past decades religious conflict has become an almost standard ingredient of conflicts around the world. Examples abound, such as the Iranian revolution inspired by Khomeiny or the Muslim opposition against the USSR invasion of Afghanistan. Especially since 2001, the percentage of religious conflicts as compared to overall conflicts is on the rise. Conflicts that focus on identity issues, such as those in Tibet, Sri Lanka, or Sudan, have a strong religious component. The addition of religious sentiments to violent conflicts creates, especially in the case of separatist conflicts, dangerous situations. Religion and separatism form an explosive mixture, just like the combination of religious fears with nationalist sentiments. The explosive affiliation of the Serbian Orthodox Church with Serbian nationalism during the leadership of Milosevic illustrates this point. As Harff and Gurr (2004, p. 31) observed, "Religious differences create a special intensity in conflicts between peoples when a dominant group attempt to impose rules based on its religious beliefs on others." Throughout the ages people have struggled—often violently—with incompatible positions on their deepest convictions. Today, an explosive worldwide conflict develops around Islam and its holy scripture, the Qu'ran. Those who attack Islam and its faithful and those who defend that religion are engaged in a dangerous spiral of hostility.

As a result of a great deal of negative media attention focused on Islam, around the world many people make an automatic link between this religion and violence. However, doing so ignores the fact that Christians also engage in violence and terrorist acts, such as the 1995 bombing of the Alfred P. Murrah Federal Building in Oklahoma City (Harff & Gurr, 2004, p. 168). There are violent Christian movements, such as the Reconstructionist Movement and the Christian Identity Organization in the United States. Furthermore, for many years Northern Ireland was a battleground between two warring Christian groups.

Extreme religious movements can engage in mass destruction of others or even their own members (collective suicide), and such movements pose—even within democracies—grave dangers, especially when they feel threatened. Examples include the Rashtriya Swayamsevak Sangh in India, the Gush Emunim in Israel, the Branch Davidians in the United States, and the Mahdi Army directed by Muqtada al-Sadr in Iraq. Moreover, religious conflicts are often intrareligious conflicts, such as between the Sunnis and Shias in Islam. There is a long history of conflicts within existing religions that did lead to the establishment of new religions, like Janism, which emerged from a conflict with the Brahman priest-hood in Hinduism. Also, within these new religions, strong divisions developed, like Hinayan Buddhism versus Mahayana Buddhism; Sikhism being divided into the Quietistic Group and the Militaristic Group; and

Confucianism being opposed by Taoism. There are also divisions in both Judaism and Islam. Christianity itself is incredibly divided into multiple mainstream institutions, including the Eastern Orthodox Church, the Roman Catholic Church, and the various churches that came out of the Reformation. And hundreds of small sects can then be added to these divisions. What's more, from its early beginnings, there were serious conflicts within Christianity. At different times, Christians escalated conflicts into destructive measures that ranged from excommunications to burning people whom they saw as heretics at the stake.

Conflict in the sense of dispute is inherent to religion. Although such disputes may be couched in theological terms, the real bones of contention were often the exercise and distribution of power as well as social control. At the core of religious thought is often the notion of "truth," which is inherently divisive and creates deep antagonisms between the believers and the nonbelievers, who hold different conceptions of truth. If one's religious truth is threatened, the essence of the believer's identity is attacked and, thus, will have to be defended, if necessary, even with violence.

THE RECURRENCE OF LETHAL COLLECTIVE CONFLICT IN CONTEMPORARY HISTORY

The mixture of resource conflicts, identity conflicts, and urban conflicts creates great potential for escalating evil. In the light of this observation, it is important to review the arguments that are conventionally used to contest the claim that the recurrence of collective violence in established democracies remains always possible.

One central argument is that democracies do not go to war with other democracies. This argument was already invalidated with the events around the Weimar Republic. The lesson of Weimar is that democracy in itself offers no protection against warfare.[8] Furthermore, even if one could argue that democracies do not fight wars against each other, they do fight wars against countries they deem to be nondemocratic, such as Vietnam, Grenada, Afghanistan, or Iraq.

Another argument defends the improbability that democracies are sites of violent conflict. On the contrary, however, the potential for contagion—and thus the proliferation of conflict—is actually particularly great in open, democratic societies, where conflicts are more easily out in the open, where more people know about them, and where more people can be mobilized to join in acting on them. This, in fact, renders democratic societies very vulnerable to the escalation of violent conflict, and this is certainly the case when democratically elected leaders manage to mobilize (perceived) ethnicity. The ethnic card has been used in conflicts in the former Soviet republics, Bosnia-Herzegovina, Croatia, Moldavia, Azerbaijan, Georgia, Tajikistan, Macedonia, Cyprus, and Northern Ireland. The Bretons use it in France, as do the Welsh and Scots in Britain.

The popular argument that democracy and violence are incompatible was often voiced by U.S. secretary of state Condoleezza Rice, UN secretary general Kofi Annan, and British foreign secretary Jack Straw. Yet another lesson from Weimar is that a democratic country can transform into an extremist country that uses lethal violence against the groups it targets for elimination. Moreover, there is a great deal of violence in democratic countries such as Israel and Turkey. Additionally, the world's largest democracy, India, is involved in violent practices in Kashmir. The United States has practiced violent terror in many of its enemy-states and has combined democratic institutions with violence in Guantánamo Bay. Furthermore, in 1993 the events in Waco, Texas, demonstrated that democratic society and religious violence are not mutually exclusive.

Consequently, the democratic nature of a society does not hamper its ability to involve itself in massive violent destruction and the killing of other nations' citizens, as the cases of the United States in Iraq, the Netherlands in Afghanistan, or Israel in Gaza demonstrate. It needs also to be considered that—ironically—demands for democratization (like in Myanmar) can lead to strong repression and massive violence.

Moreover, it is in Western democracies where scientists have developed the most dangerous weapons of mass destruction, and so far, a Western democracy has been the only political system that has massively killed civilians by using the nuclear bomb.

Finally, the "politics of violent intervention" is fully accepted by most UN member states, including Western mature democracies. Humanitarian intervention always implies the risk—or better the certainty—of killing civilians because, increasingly, the Western interventionists use weapons (bombardments) that are more dangerous for civilians than they are for soldiers.

Another argument claims that the capitalist arrangement of the economy in democratic societies is more inclined toward peace than toward war.

As Klaus Jürgen Gantzel wrote,

Capitalism, in the end, brings peace.... The process of creating the conditions for capitalism is always accompanied by war and other forms of violence, but capitalism itself tends to non-violent forms of conflicts because violence is counter-productive to its economic, political and social interests. (1997, p. 140)

It is certainly true that an element of pacification is essential for mercantile societies—trouble is bad for business. Capitalism, however, divides people into rich versus poor, thus fueling the luxury fever that can only be satisfied by small numbers of people. Its politics of privatization erode communal responsibility and solidarity. Commercial motives are forever in conflict with moral considerations. Capitalist societies are "class" societies, and the divided classes have an inherently conflictual relationship. And, as we have seen, conflicts can escalate!

A characteristic of democratic societies that have experienced little or no warfare in recent decades is that the use of violence is the exclusive prerogative of the state. This monopolization of violence by the state (Elias, 1982) is undermined in capitalist societies by the outsourcing of violence to private parties. Prison systems, surveillance, and control tasks are privatized, and all offer potential for escalating conflict. Even though states may refrain from waging wars against each other, they are doubtlessly increasingly involved in internal warfare.

Even if the "war and democracy" or "war and capitalism" arguments would hold, they still do not exclude that democracy and capitalism are the targets of violent destruction. What's more, democratic-capitalist countries can be the targets of acts of mass destruction, as 9/11 as well as the London and Madrid bombings convincingly demonstrated. Moreover, democracies are certainly not beyond the use of symbolic violence against targeted individuals and groups.

Another argument often used is that over time we have become less violent and that this trend will continue. People are today probably less violent than in earlier times. They have done away with the ritual of human sacrifices to obtain favors from the gods. There are no longer people burning at the stake. There is no more medieval quartering of people—although the recent wars in Iraq, Chechnya, and Bosnia-Herzegovia have exposed the world to gruesome decapitations. There is no more stoning for adultery—although recently in Nigeria and Algeria, leaders have pleaded for its return, together with flogging and amputation. Abu Ghraib was a horrendous incident, but in the Middle Ages, it would have been standard practice, and few if any people would have protested. The few who did protest were broken on the wheel, much to the amusement of ordinary folks and members of the nobility who considered watching violent torture an amusing pastime. Indeed, we do not go to the village marketplace to enjoy beheadings but instead stay home and watch Mel Gibson on television. That is the fruit of the civilizing process.

A final argument against the possibility of the return of massive destruction of human dignity is that human beings learn from history. However, that is historically an unlikely argument because humans characteristically make the same errors time and again. Barbara Tuchman has provided overwhelming empirical evidence of this in her book *March of Folly,* chronicling human insensitivity to error: "Persisting in error is the problem.... to recognize error, to cut losses, to alter course, is the most repugnant option in government" (1984, p. 481).

CONCLUSION

As the Peace and Conflict Study of 2010 (Hewitt et al.) concluded: "Armed conflict will be a persistent feature of the geopolitical landscape for the foreseeable future" (p. 6).

Thus, the risk of escalating evil continues to be a reality in modern societies. In order to confront this, we need to explore how the spiral from disagreement toward destruction can in time be halted. Throughout this book, the mass media of information and entertainment have been presented as important vehicles in amplifying the crucial phases of the escalation spiral. In the next chapter, I propose an alert system that realizes a timely intervention when media are inciting their audiences to commit evil.

CHAPTER 7

INTERNATIONAL MEDIA ALERT SYSTEM (IMAS)

⟿

CRIMES AGAINST HUMANITY

As was suggested in chapter 1, the grand-scale perpetration of crimes against humanity forms the dramatic core of identity conflicts. Crimes against humanity transgress most cultures' taboos, such as the murder or torture of defenseless men, women, and children. Among the crimes against humanity—as defined by international law—are murder and extermination of civilian populations, genocide, and apartheid.

Crimes against humanity are acts that make the perpetrator an enemy of the human species. In legal terms, the perpetrator is "hostis humani generis." According to international law, perpetrators can be state institutions, private organizations, or individuals. The Charter of the International Military Tribunal of Nuremberg gives the following definition (in Article 6):

Crimes against Humanity, namely murder, extermination, enslavement, deportation, and other inhumane acts committed against any civilian population, before or during the war, or persecutions on political, racial or religious grounds in execution of or in connection with any crime within the jurisdiction of the Tribunal, whether or not in violation of the domestic law of the country where perpetrated.

An important element of the definition is that states can commit such crimes against their own population—"against any civilian population." Also essential is that a state cannot appeal to national legislation for justification: "whether or not in violation of the domestic law." Crimes against humanity are characterized by the force with which they undermine the experience of human dignity of the victims and deny their victims' integrity and autonomy. Therefore, if perpetrators of these crimes are not held accountable and punished, the crime committed is not recognized as such and is thus denied, which then robs the victims of their dignity yet again.

Although impunity is characteristic of the treatment of those who commit violations of human rights, under international law, the members of the international community are obligated to prosecute crimes against humanity. War crimes and crimes against humanity, including the incitement to these criminal acts, must be punished.

In 1996 the international community began—finally—to take this matter seriously, and the General Assembly of the UN decided on a concrete agenda for the establishment of an international criminal court. In July 1998 the United Nations convened an international diplomatic conference in Rome that produced a treaty establishing the permanent International Criminal Court (ICC), which is charged to deal with war crimes and crimes against humanity. In accordance with existing treaties, the court will have the mandate to prosecute genocide, and Article 25 of the Statute of the ICC provides that the crime of genocide includes the incitement to genocide.

However, serious obstacles remain that hinder the ICC from functioning effectively. Important UN member states, such as the United States, have not agreed to participate in the court. Such countries object on the grounds that they do not want to bring their citizens before an international tribunal. Actually, most governments would most probably have great problems standing trial if they themselves were responsible for crimes against humanity. Another problem concerns the question of who should be prosecuted: political leaders only or also members of the lower echelons? A problem with the latter is that often they appeal to orders from higher authorities. The Charter of the International Military Tribunal of Nuremberg formulated for these cases the rule that "the fact that the Defendant acted pursuant to order of his Government or of a superior shall not free him from responsibility." When faced with these cases, the tribunal questioned whether the accused could have acted differently (Roht-Arriaza, 1995, p. 65).

Once the perpetrators of crimes against humanity are brought to justice, however, it usually is too late for the victims. Because of this, spotting and subsequently exposing, as early as possible, public expressions of elimination beliefs is of the utmost importance.

EARLY ALERT

An International Media Alert System is needed that monitors media contents in areas of conflict. This system would provide an "early warning" where and when media set the climate for crimes against humanity and begin to motivate people to kill others.[1]

The legal motivation behind an International Media Alert System is the extension of the "responsibility to protect" (Evans, 2008) to the protection of potential victims against incitement to atrocities during the preparatory phase of genocide. This "responsibility to protect" principle overrules the principle of national sovereignty that has prevailed in international relations since the Peace of Westphalia in 1648. Its formal adoption by the UN in 2005 makes it possible to intervene in the internal genocidal affairs of a national government.

However, if this intervention takes place once the atrocities have begun, the international community is too late. Although there are currently situations in which the responsibility to protect could and should be applied, like in Darfur, there remains considerable hesitation in various countries about their responsibility to protect, especially countries in Africa, Asia, and Latin America that fear—and possibly correctly—that it could be abused to justify military interventions. This does, however, provide an extra argument for the application of this principle during the agitation phase of conflict escalation. At that point in time, no military interventions or economic sanctions are needed. In 2007, during the outbreak of violence in Kenya, the principle of responsibility to protect was implemented (largely effectively) without military means and through international diplomacy and political mediation.[2]

ELIMINATION BELIEFS

Although crimes can be committed without apparent motivation, exercising gross violence at a grand scale—as in crimes against humanity—requires motivating beliefs. In order for people to commit such crimes, they need to believe that their violent acts are right and that the victims need to be eliminated.

Crimes against humanity often take place in situations in which the media take part in systematically disseminating propagandistic misinformation about the "others." This propaganda aims to justify socially and/or physically eliminating an out-group. Members of such groups are often first targeted as "socially undesirable." They are publicly ridiculed, insulted, and provoked (often in the media). When the harassments are put into action, the victims are beaten and killed. In the propagation of "elimination beliefs," the "others" are dehumanized, whereas the superiority of one's own group is emphasized. The propagandists convincingly suggest to their audiences that the "others" pose fundamental threats to the security and well-being of society and that the only effective means of escaping this threat is to eliminate this great danger. They then present the use of violence in this process as inevitable and, thus, not only acceptable but absolutely necessary.

The elimination beliefs that motivate people to kill each other are not part of the human genetic constitution. They are social constructs, which, therefore, need social institutions for their dissemination. Such institutions include religious communities, schools, families, and the mass media. In this context, it is striking that before various Truth Commissions convened in countries after they had experienced periods of prolonged violence (e.g., during the period 1971–1996 in Uganda, Bolivia, Argentina, Uruguay, Zimbabwe, the Philippines, Chile, Chad, El Salvador, Ethiopia, and Haiti), no hate speech propagandists were interrogated or sentenced. The reason behind this may be that the dissemination of propaganda—however hateful—through mass media does not imply the use of physical violence. The difficult question this poses is whether propagating such ideas and beliefs can be construed as a crime against humanity and whether restricting hate speech could violate the fundamental right to free speech. Can justifiable choices be made between two evils—the evil of limiting free speech and the evil of harmful incitement?

In his book *Hitler's Willing Executioners,* Daniel Goldhagen wrote that

> Germans' anti-Semitic beliefs about Jews were the central causal agent of the Holocaust.... Not economic hardship, not the coercive means of a totalitarian state, not social psychological pressure, not invariable

psychological propensities, but ideas about Jews that were pervasive in Germany, and had been for decades, induced ordinary Germans to kill unarmed, defenseless Jewish men, women and children by the thousands, systematically and without pity. (1997, p. 9).

In attempts to explain the genocide in Nazi Germany, historians and social scientists often gloss over the fact that anti-Semitic propaganda played a central role (Goldhagen, 1997, p. 478). Goldhagen argued that precisely the belief—which was shared by numerous ordinary Germans—that Jews deserved to die was decisive. The belief that Jews were fundamentally evil, subhuman, and dangerous made genocide inevitable and acceptable. The story of the Holocaust—as well as other atrocities in history—demonstrates that ordinary people are capable of actively and enthusiastically mass-slaughtering their fellow human beings once they are ideologically motivated to do so.

Because crimes against humanity are unthinkable without elimination beliefs, the institutional carriers of such beliefs (such as mass media that propagate beliefs that support genocide) have to be treated as perpetrators of crimes against humanity.

INTERNATIONAL LAW

There are relevant provisions in international law that address the incitement to violence. The Convention on the Prevention and Punishment of the Crime of Genocide (United Nations 1948a) provides in Article 3 that genocide and direct and public incitement to genocide are punishable under international law. Article 4 states that persons committing acts mentioned in Article 3 "shall be punished, whether they are constitutionally responsible rulers, public officials or private individuals."

The International Convention on the Elimination of All Forms of Racial Discrimination provides in Article 4.a: "punishable by law all dissemination of ideas based upon racial superiority or hatred, incitement to racial discrimination, as well as all acts of violence or incitement to such acts" (United Nations 1966a).

In international human rights law, the prohibition of discrimination is considered binding law (Hannikainen, 1988, pp. 467–489). The International Covenant on Civil and Political Rights (United Nations 1966b) provides in Article 20, para. 2: "Any advocacy of national, racial or religious hatred that constitutes incitement to discrimination, hostility or violence shall be prohibited by law."

Prosecution and Trial

In the case of serious violations of the norms of human dignity, a basic principle of law should be maintained: Prosecution and trial should follow. Already in 1625 the legal scholar Hugo de Groot developed in his famous study "De Iure Belli ac Pacis" the principle that those who violate international law should be prosecuted and extradited. In the development of legal thought about international crimes, two trends can be observed: Jurisdiction shifts from possible to mandatory prosecution by states, and the number of violations that should be prosecuted increases.

What effects can we realistically expect from prosecuting and sentencing the disseminators of incitement to crimes against humanity? Will it deter people from this behavior? Will the threat of criminal prosecution and prison terms stop prohibited expressions? Because such expressions are motivated by strong convictions and fears, and because they represent the basic interests that people pursue, it is more likely that—if repressed—these expressions will go underground rather than disappear. Therefore, the advantage of their absence from the public sphere has to be balanced against their uncontrollable presence in societal twilight. Whether societies can ever eliminate strong ideas and opinions without eliminating their carriers is questionable. However, doing so would make the perpetrators victims of the crimes they perpetrate.

Deterrence may have positive effects if perpetrators know and accept that their beliefs are illegal and criminal. However, in the case of incitement to genocide, the perpetrators will often be convinced (and supported in such conviction by their governments) that their actions are desirable and necessary. This renders punishment meaningless.

Can criminal prosecution have an educational effect and change undesirable behavior? In daily life, we encounter loads of prohibitions that tell us what not to do. For these rules to work, however, those upon whom they are imposed must understand and accept their sense. But can it be explained to the disseminators of elimination beliefs that censoring them is socially meaningful?

Can we expect a reconciliatory effect of prosecution and trial? In treaties concerning violations of human rights the option of amnesty is not explicitly prohibited, but there is within UN human rights institutions a clear trend to deny amnesty in cases of serious violations. The belief that amnesty would strengthen the common climate of impunity that is so characteristic for the current international human rights regime motivates this trend (Roht-Arriaza, 1995, p. 59). Forgiveness and reconciliation imply that perpetrators escape their responsibility and accountability for committing evil. Crimes against humanity touch on the essence of human dignity, and the incitement to such crimes takes away the humanity of the victims. The measure of punishment should make apparent how strongly a society condemns the violation of human dignity.

The International Military Tribunal of Nuremberg

In 1946 the International Military Tribunal of Nuremberg (IMT) denounced racist propaganda as a crime against humanity. The IMT recognized the essential significance of a genocidal ideology and established criminal responsibility for its dissemination. The tribunal found Julius Streicher, member of the Nazi party since 1921 as well as editor (1923–1933) and publisher (1923–1945) of *Der Stürmer* (an anti-Semitic weekly), guilty of crimes against humanity. Over the course of 25 years, Streicher had incited Germans to actively persecute Jews. In *Der Stürmer,* he preached that the Jewish race should be eliminated. He described Jews as parasites that had to be destroyed. The tribunal concluded that Streicher's incitement to murder and elimination constituted a crime against humanity and, thus, sentenced him to death. According to the tribunal, Streicher had "injected into the minds of thousands of Germans" a "poison" that caused them to support the National Socialist policy of Jewish persecution and extermination. The IMT sentence provided important case law for recognizing the incitement to genocide as a crime.

Recognizing this is, however, not as easy a matter as Nuremberg demonstrated. The court also dealt with the case against Hans Fritzsche, a high officer in the Nazi propaganda department, radio propagandist, and one of the men responsible for broadcasting anti-Semitic messages. The members of the court—with the exception of the Soviet judge—did not find him guilty of incitement to genocide. Though his statements were anti-Semitic, he did not explicitly call for the elimination of Jews. However, Fritzsche did fully support the Nazi policies and their goals, which included the persecution and elimination of Jews.

The International Tribunal on Genocide in Rwanda

The United Nations established the International Criminal Tribunal for Rwanda in November 1994; in 1995 it was located in Arsuha, Tanzania.

The trial of the court against incitement to genocide began in October 2000. In August 2004 three life sentences were requested. The accused were Ferdinand Nahimana, cofounder of the radio station Radio Télévision Libre des Mille Collines (RTLM, see chapter 2); Jean Bosco Barayagwiza, leader of the RTLM; and Hassan Ngeze, who founded and, since 1990, was editor-in-chief of the newspaper *Kangura,* which was probably the most well-known newspaper during the period of the genocide. All three defendants were found guilty, and on December 3, 2003, Nahimama and Ngeze were sentenced to life in prison and Barayagwiza to thirty-five years in prison. They appealed the sentences, but in 2008 and 2009 these were denied final conclusions.

The charges against the defendants included the public incitement to commit genocide. The judgment of the trial chamber states that

> This case raises important principles concerning the role of the media, which have not been addressed at the level of international criminal justice since Nuremberg. The power of the media to create and destroy fundamental human values comes with great responsibility. Those who control such media are accountable for its consequences.

In the case against Hassan Ngeze, the court found that *Kangura* published in December 1990 his so-called Ten Commandments in an article entitled "Appeal to the Conscience of the Hutu." The introduction of this article warned readers:

> The enemy is still there, among us, and is biding his time to try again, at a more propitious moment, to decimate us. Therefore, Hutu, wherever you may be, wake up! Be firm and vigilant. Take all necessary measures to deter the enemy from launching a fresh attack.

These Ten Commandments exhorted the Hutu to wake up "now or never" and become aware of a new Hutu ideology, with roots in and in defense of the 1959 revolution. It referenced the historical servitude of the Hutu, and readers were urged to "be prepared to defend themselves against this scourge." The ninth commandment concludes, "The Hutu must be firm and vigilant towards their common Tutsi enemy."

The chamber found that the "Appeal to the Conscience of the Hutu" and the Ten Commandments of the Hutu conveyed contempt and hatred for the Tutsi ethnic group and for Tutsi women in particular as enemy agents. The "Appeal to the Conscience of the Hutu" portrayed the

Tutsi as a ruthless enemy, determined to conquer the Hutu, and called on the Hutu to take all necessary measures to stop the enemy.

In the cases against Nahimama and Barayagwiza (on RTLM), the court found

> that RTLM broadcasts engaged in ethnic stereotyping in a manner that promoted contempt and hatred for the Tutsi population. RTLM broadcasts called on listeners to seek out and take up arms against the enemy. The enemy was identified as the RPF, the Inkotanyi, the Inyenzi, and their accomplices, all of whom were effectively equated with the Tutsi ethnic group by the broadcasts. After 6 April 1994, the virulence and the intensity of RTLM broadcasts propagating ethnic hatred and calling for violence increased. These broadcasts called explicitly for the extermination of the Tutsi ethnic group.

According to the judgment of the trial chamber,

> both before and after 6 April 1994, RTLM broadcast the names of Tutsi individuals and their families, as well as Hutu political opponents. In some cases, these people were subsequently killed, and the Chamber finds that to varying degrees their deaths were causally linked to the broadcast of their names. RTLM also broadcast messages encouraging Tutsi civilians to come out of hiding and to return home or to go to the roadblocks, where they were subsequently killed in accordance with the direction of subsequent RTLM broadcasts tracking their movement. Radio was the medium of mass communication with the broadest reach in Rwanda. The Chamber finds that RTLM broadcasts exploited the history of Tutsi privilege and Hutu disadvantage, and the fear of armed insurrection, to mobilize the population, whipping them into a frenzy of hatred and violence that was directed largely against the Tutsi ethnic group. The Interahamwe and other militia listened to RTLM and acted on the information that was broadcast by RTLM. RLTM actively encouraged them to kill, relentlessly sending the message that the Tutsi were the enemy and had to be eliminated once and for all.

In its charge, the trial chamber found that "RTLM broadcasts engaged in ethnic stereotyping in a manner that promoted contempt and hatred for the Tutsi population and called on listeners to seek out and take up arms against the enemy."

In its reflection on the international jurisprudence related to direct and public incitement to genocide, the trial chamber concluded that

Editors and publishers have generally been held responsible for the media they control. In determining the scope of this responsibility, the importance of intent, that is the purpose of the communications they channel, emerges from the jurisprudence. The actual language used in the media has often been cited as an indicator of intent.

According to the chamber, the jurisprudence on incitement also highlights the importance of taking context into account when considering the potential impact of expression: "Other factors relating to context that emerge from the jurisprudence, particularly that of the European Court of Human Rights, include the importance of protecting political expression, particularly the expression of opposition views and criticism of the government." Of particular interest in the chamber's reflection is the consideration that "the international jurisprudence does not include any specific causation requirement linking the expression at issue with the demonstration of a direct effect." This means that the crime of genocide is inchoate: It is a crime even though the substantive offense is not completed. This is allows for the possibility to prosecute in cases of incitement to genocide without establishing the real effects of such incitement.

The chamber made a distinction between crimes of persecution, as crimes of impact, and crimes of incitement, as crimes of intent. Just like the writing of Nazi propagandist Julius Streicher,

> the virulent writings of *Kangura* and the incendiary broadcasts of RTLM functioned in the same way, conditioning the Hutu population and creating a climate of harm, as evidenced in part by the extermination and genocide that followed. Similarly, the activities of the CDR, a Hutu political party that demonized the Tutsi population as the enemy, generated fear and hatred that created the conditions for extermination and genocide in Rwanda.[3]

In its reference to the jurisprudence of the European Court of Human Rights, the chamber expressed a concern about the balance between the responsibility to intervene in the provision of information and the responsibility to protect media's fundamental freedom.

THE FREEDOM OF EXPRESSION

Free speech is a fundamental human right. International, regional, and national human rights provisions open the possibility for limitation and derogation but—given the essential nature of this right—the limits cannot be too elastic. Human rights are universal in the sense that all people matter. No one can be excluded from enjoying these rights. Everyone can claim the right to free speech. However, this also means that everyone needs to respect and recognize everyone else's right to this same claim. Human rights work because of reciprocity, and thus inciting acts that destroy these rights for others is unacceptable. The person who disseminates elimination belief denies others the right to freedom of expression and, thus, loses his or her claim to the protection of this right. Claiming a right to freedom implies the willingness to grant others the right to also exercise this freedom (Raes, 1995, p. 59).[4]

Ironically, elimination beliefs are usually not disseminated in political environments that protect free speech. Freedom of information does not normally lead to inciting people to kill others. On the contrary, incitement to crimes against humanity is often found in situations of confusion and fear, when journalists are afraid to speak up and governments exercise great pressures on the media. In countries such as Rwanda and the former Yugoslavia, the government systematically censored the media. The professional autonomy of media needs to be robustly secured in order to protect them against manipulation by the perpetrators of crimes against humanity. Protecting the freedom of information does raise the difficult question of where the border lies when speech that may be immoral needs legal protection lest media are exposed to the slippery road of censorship.

IS "HATE SPEECH" A CRIME?

International law (Article 20 of the 1966 International Covenant on Civil and Political Rights) provides that governments are obliged to prohibit any advocacy of national, racial, or religious hatred that constitutes incitement to discrimination, hostility, or violence. This provision, however, does not make hate speech a criminal offense under international law; rather, it suggests that national legislators create laws against hate speech. A great number of countries around the world, including Rwanda, have domestic laws that ban advocacy of discriminatory hate, recognizing the danger it represents and the harm it causes.[5]

The chamber in the Rwandan trial considered that, in light of well-established principles of international and domestic law, hate speech that expresses ethnic and other forms of discrimination violates the norm of customary international law prohibiting discrimination. It stated that

"Within this norm of customary law, the prohibition of advocacy of discrimination and incitement to violence is increasingly important as the power of the media to harm is increasingly acknowledged."[6]

This raises the essential question of whether hate speech should indeed be prosecuted under penal law. Does hate speech imply that people are incited to commit a crime? In Dutch criminal law, for example (Article 137, d), incitement to violence, discrimination, and hate are brought together. However, incitement to violence and discrimination implies that people are incited to commit crimes. Hate, however, cannot be legally punished. Hate is not a crime but rather an extremely negative emotion. Hate is a very unpleasant, undesirable, and possibly dangerous emotion, but, much like love, it is a very human emotion. To incite people to hate fellow human beings is indecent or even abject, but people are free to hate each other. The dividing lines between hatred and related emotions, such as strong dislike, disgust, or fear, are fuzzy, and therefore, prohibiting hate speech is very risky because it could lead to arbitrary restriction of free speech.

Moreover, there is the real danger—as has happened in Africa—that governments abuse hate speech provisions to curb the media. Critical media can be restrained by accusing them of hate speech. The Committee to Protect Journalists has documented many such cases. The accusation of ethnic division has been used in Rwanda (in 2003 forward) to silence critical journalists.

Focusing on the prosecution of incitement to genocide would be more productive. Contrary to the emotion of hate, elimination is a criminal act, and inciting people to criminal acts is considered worldwide an act that merits punishment. With regard to the public incitement to elimination, important international legal precedents have been set, and as a result, incitement to elimination can be successfully prosecuted. Furthermore, identifying and recognizing "elimination" texts is also likely be somewhat easier and less contested than evaluating hate texts.

If hate speech is criminalized, the prosecution will have to provide convincing evidence of discriminatory or violent acts that were caused by feelings of hatred. This will often be an impossible task because it requires comprehensive, longitudinal social research, which, at present, is not available.

In prosecuting hate speech, there are enormous problems with the interpretation of the expressions used by the accused. Those texts only rarely call explicitly for people to hate each other, and therefore, this appeal to hate needs to be based on an interpretation of expressions, which is necessarily subjective. Expressions are always open to a variety of interpretations, which will be inspired by personal preferences and dislikes of prosecutors and judges.

Therefore, to avoid arbitrariness, not only content but also intent and context need to be weighed. There needs to be evidence that the speaker intends to promote criminal acts, could foresee that the expressions would lead to criminal acts, and could foresee the illegal consequences of his speech. There also needs to be evidence that the societal environment was receptive to the understanding that the hate speech called for criminal acts, the speaker had sufficient authority to incite people to hatred, there were no other speakers to balance the expressions of the speaker, and the audience did interpret the expressions in accordance with the intentions of the speaker.[7]

Therefore, in preparing for an international media early warning system (IMAS), it is an important observation that the much-needed international support requires a common ground with different parties, such as free speech advocates. Thus, even as hate speech prohibition is contested, the sentencing of the Arusha court on incitement to genocide has been called by the *New York Times* (in an editorial comment of December 5, 2003) "rightly decided," "welcome," and "no threat to journalistic free speech." Therefore, the primary focus of the IMAS project should be on media contents that represent forms of incitement that are punishable under international law. These include the incitement to kill members of a national, ethnic, racial, or religious group or to cause serious bodily or mental harm to members of such groups.[8]

RESEARCH NEEDED

The establishment of the IMAS project would need some essential lines of research. A key topic for media research would be how to design reliable and valid methods of content analysis for media monitoring. Which messages constitute incitement to genocide or violence against target groups? What are the characteristics of such messages? How can we differentiate from messages that may offend target groups but do not incite harm against them? What constitutes harm? A particularly challenging issue in this context is the definition of mental harm: When do media messages cause serious damage to people's mental well-being?[9]

A key area for legal research would be the current provisions in international law. Are they adequate? What would constitute more appropriate and effective formulations? What can the International Criminal

Court do? How can cases be brought to the court? Who has the right to stand in the court? How should groups be represented?

Free speech studies would focus on the relation between incitement to genocide speech, hate speech, and free speech. Which modalities of speech are covered by the right to freedom of expression? How can restrictions of free speech be legally justified? Such studies would also address the feasibility of a phased system of warning. What should be done in cases when the media begin to encourage the escalation spiral without explicitly using punishable expressions?

Studies on media professionalism would inquire how the operation of a media alert system relates to the professional independence of journalists. Furthermore, it prompts the question: How should the profession deal with the distinction between propaganda and journalism?

CONCLUSION

The dissemination of "elimination beliefs" that will eventually lead to the collective destruction of human dignity constitutes a crime against humanity. Alerting the international community—through media monitoring—whenever and wherever this crime is committed is, therefore, crucial. The International Media Alert System would primarily focus its monitoring on media contents that intend to incite people to eliminate targeted groups and, more broadly, on contents that lead to the escalation of conflicts and, thus, mass violence.

CHAPTER 8

LEARNING FROM ALBERT CAMUS[1]

✎

"Modern chimpanzees are not merely fellow time-travellers and evolutionary relatives, but surprisingly excellent models of our direct ancestors.... Chimpanzee-like violence preceded and paved the way for human war, making modern humans the dazed survivors of a continuous, 5-million-year habit of lethal aggression."

Richard Wrangham and Dale Peterson (1996)

In the preceding chapters, I argued that we need to search for ways to prevent high-complexity conflicts from escalating into the evil of the destruction of human dignity. I discussed the role of the mass media as facilitators in the spiral of escalation and developed proposals for processes of de-escalation. All this now raises the question of what can be expected.

Can we tame evil? We can accept the taming of evil as a realistic proposition, provided we see this as temporary relief. Seeing this as a perpetual situation, however, as a possible end-goal of human history, seems unrealistic and even dangerous.

According to the writings of social thinkers such as Joachim di Fiori, Lessing, Hegel, and Comte, as well as contemporary information revolution authors such as Alvin Toffler, Nicholas Negroponte, and Bill Gates, history proceeds in progressive steps: Through enlightenment, rationality, and, particularly, science and technology, humanity is on the road toward harmony and peace. This is a myth of human progress, and it was exploded by Auschwitz and Hiroshima. There is no linear progressive process; history is circular and revolves continually around the same core—the human possibility. The suggestion of moral progress is misleading. The human species is locked into the recurring waves of gross immoral conduct and refined moral reflection.

Inhumanity is part of the human phenomenon. It is a human possibility. The human being is a species in disequilibrium. Unlike other animals, humans are ex-centric beings that experience confrontations between their cultural constructs and their natural inclinations. Moral philosophy has always struggled with the gap between people's moral aspirations and their real actions. Solutions to this "moral divide" can be sought in an appeal to God to assist humanity, in the improvement of human moral capacity, or in the attempt to downsize moral claims. However, leaving it to God to sort out the "moral divide" means that humans give up on their agency and their responsibility and, thus, deny very basic human capacities. The project of improving humanity has often ended up in disaster. Whether inspired by Enlightenment ideals or eugenic practices, there exists always the risk of projects that breed the superior and weed out the inferior. It is a returning point of doctrine in a variety of fundamentalisms (whether Stalinism, Fascism, Maoism, or extreme Islamism) that extermination is sanctioned insofar as it advances humanity's improvement. Adjusting moral demands to human nature is an equally unattractive project. It would almost certainly mean that we end up with the lowest possible standard of achievement and would ignore the possibility that humans can transcend their innate inadequacies.

We have to search for the maximum equilibrium between moral claim and moral capacity, and we may achieve this only temporarily. There is little use in searching for the lasting, permanent solution to the "moral divide." The balance we seek will be temporary.

Human history is a succession of waves of morality and immorality. Humanity and inhumanity are part of the human condition. There is no watertight schism between the forces of good and evil. The expectation that evil—usually represented by the others—can be eliminated is a dangerous delusion that refuses to accept that the inhuman is part of all human beings, irrespective of their moral ambitions and pretenses.

We have to be realistic about our flaws and failures as a species and be prepared for recurrent immorality. In our uncertain walk toward the future, we may experience failures that will be followed by incredibly beautiful moments when moral claims and moral capacity are a perfect match.

UTOPIANISM

Peace and war are temporal phenomena. The vision of everlasting peace is a fallacious utopian construct. John Gray (2007, p. 195) claimed that "The belief that humanity is moving toward a condition in which there will be no more conflict over the nature of government is not only delusive but also dangerous." As Gray argued, this belief is dangerous because it does not prepare people for the very real possibility of intractable conflict. Moreover, eternal peace would imply the elimination of differences and, thus, the end of democratic processes. Andreas Behnke (2008) has argued that an idealist conception of Kant's notion of "eternal peace" would mean the graveyard of the political.

Does this imply that adopting a crude form of cyclical thinking is necessary? Does this mean we need to go back to concepts of time that guided the Pythagoreans, Stoics, Babylonians, Egyptians, Aztecs, or Mayans; or Vedic Hindu culture; or Tantric Buddhism? Do we have to think about intractable conflict in the Nietzschean sense of the eternal recurrence of the same? Do we perpetually have to relive Groundhog Day?[2] Or, would it be better to conceive of human conflict from a linear time perspective? Or would this imply the adoption of equally crude models in which history develops along a straight line from creation to the day of judgment?

The distinction between the cyclical and the linear is too artificial to be useful. What's more, it militates against our daily life experience (Holl, 1985). Our lives follow a linear structure from birth to death, and yet, throughout life, we experience cyclical patterns: so many feelings, so many déjà vu moments, such perpetual repetition, so much more of the same! Just think of the cyclical patterns of holidays, birthdays, the annual holiday family dinner, walking the dog. Also, between the beginning and the end of our lives, we experience in many parts of the world the cyclical movement of the seasons. However much the narrations of the Abrahamic religions (Judaism, Christianity, and Islam) tell us about linear developments from a finite beginning, Ecclesiastes 1:9 reminds us, "That which has been is that which will be. And that which has been done is that which will be done. So there is nothing new under the sun."

Conversely, if we believed time was only cyclical, we would exclude the possibility of human improvement. This would make such activities as promoting and protecting human rights futile. Learning would be meaningless. Forgiveness and reconciliation would be senseless categories. Writing a book on preventing the escalation of evil would be an utter waste of time matched only by reading it.

Humans are sense-making animals. It is unlikely that other animals (even the primates) are as perplexed by living and dying as humans are. The human species is forever busy with finding (either in religious or secular ways) meaning for the ultimate questions about sickness, suffering, evil, death, and after death. Therefore, we create mental constructs (which may be illusions but can be true illusions), such as linearity, circularity, temporality, and eternity. We need to be mentally flexible in order to live with such paradoxes: Linearity only makes sense in combination with circularity, just like temporality and eternity belong together. Kant's notion of "eternal peace" transforms—in the light of the temporality/eternity paradox—from a dangerous utopian ideal into a useful political guide.[3] The paradox enables us to cope with the reality of regression (the psychotherapist who does not accept the regression of his clients should change jobs) and protects us against the risks of teleological vistas, whether they be positive or negative.

Another paradox is that humans are both "bricoleurs" and "engineers." Claude Lévi-Strauss made that distinction to describe the "savage mind" and the "scientific mind" (1966). The bricoleur is the multitasker who puts—piecemeal—existing things together in new ways (the "savage" mind), whereas the engineer deals with projects in a holistic way and designs new tools. The paradox is that both are needed. Taming evil requires that we tinker with whatever we can find in order to prevent the escalation of conflict. At the same time, grand designs about future possibilities are likewise required.

Should the future of conflict be conceived of in utopian terms? Reading Thomas More's 1516 work *Utopia,* it is clear that More himself knows that his utopian society is both unachievable and undesirable (More, 1984). The island, with all its orders and restrictions, is a totalitarian state. Utopian thinking is dangerous and leaves many victims in its tracks. Gray observed that "Utopian projects are by their nature unachievable" (2007, p. 17).They pursue the unrealistic dream of conflict-free societies and are often willing to make masses of people victims in order to realize such dreams. Stalin, Hitler, Mao, and Pol Pot are among the great utopists of the twentieth century. Millions of people were massacred for their ideals of a good society. Furthermore, the Peruvian Shining Path movement killed thousands of people to achieve the best possible world. Terror is an acceptable price to those who want to perfect humankind. Thus, the refusal to accept that humans are far from perfect poses grave dangers. It inspires the use of violence to improve the human condition. Whatever else may have motivated Western governments to invade Iraq and Afghanistan, these wars were also unrealistic utopian projects that aspired to impose peace and democracy by "shock and awe." The mission that equates modernity with the better human condition and then bombs the beneficiaries of the good news from great altitudes into submission is a mission that escalates inevitably toward endless wars. Ironically, such missions are usually termed "humanitarian."

Striving toward the salvation of others inevitably clashes with those who do not want to be saved or who have their own definition of a better world. The more committed the salvation missionaries are, however, the greater their moral blindness for the readiness to deploy violence against dissidents. If the utopian project aspires to end evil, then all those who stand in the way—or who are suspected to stand in the way—must be eliminated. Because people have inevitably different notions of what the end of evil means, positive utopia and elimination are inherently linked.

Utopianism has both positive and negative dimensions. The danger of the negative utopia is that it works out as a self-fulfilling prophecy. Robert K. Merton coined this term in his *Social Theory and Social Structure* (1968). He was inspired by the theorem of W. I. Thomas (1928), who stated, "If men define situations as real, they are real in their consequences." This theorem essentially proposes that views of the world influence real-life action in the world.

A prophecy or a prediction that people believe to be true (although it may be based on misinformation and rumor) affects real developments. The classical example of the self-fulfilling prophecy comes from the Greek myth of Oedipus, who kills his father and sleeps with his mother. His father, King Laius, listens to a fortune teller who warns him that his son will kill him, so he sends his newborn child to be raised somewhere by foster parents. Another prophecy tells Oedipus that he will kill his father and marry his mother, so he leaves the people he believes to be his real parents. Not knowing who his real parents are, he kills king Laius and marries the king's widow, Oedipus's mother. Taking the prophecies seriously ends with traumatic tragedy.

If people hold negative expectations about each other, they are likely to react to the others in line with their expectation, which in turn confirms the negative image the others have, who will respond in ways that confirm expectations about who they are. Eventually, all will act in ways that conform to their initial expectations.

As was argued before, the currently popular negative utopias (dystopias) regarding climate change are not particularly helpful to developing plausible scenarios for the planet's future. Society's overwhelming support for the dystopia of "global warming," for example, may hamper our ability to prepare for "global cooling" (Solomon, 2008, p. 167).

A question that needs to be raised here is whether proposing the inevitability of conflict—asserted throughout this book—is not itself a self-fulfilling prophecy, a negative utopia. Merton (1968, p. 477) wrote that a self-fulfilling prophecy begins with a "false definition of the situation." The thesis about the inevitability of disputes between people who live in different universes is based on sufficiently solid observations and could not be termed a "false definition." Furthermore, the proposition that conflict is inevitable does not announce that the escalation of conflict into evil is inevitable; rather, the spiral of escalation can be prevented. This does not argue for the positive utopia that eliminates evil, because this position would find no convincing support in human history. However, there are likewise no arguments for the negative utopia that taming evil is impossible.

REALISM

Where do we go once we liberate ourselves from utopian beliefs?

Gray (2007) argued for the acceptance of realistic thought. This sounds like an attractive position: no romanticizing about human goodness and no scare mongering the living daylights out of people. Neither optimism nor pessimism. No disillusions and no self-fulfilling prophecies. Nonetheless, there are problems with this position. Realism that rejects the human potential for change is deeply conservative. It is inspired by a strong deterministic trend that portrays the human being as, by nature, inclined to evil (Sandole, 1984, p. 39). Believing in humanity's innate evil is no different than believing in innate goodness.

It is a belief that is not supported by solid, rational arguments. Just as blind idealism makes many victims, cynical realism does not seriously care about the victims. Just like the utopists, the realists are locked up in the mental cage of their absolutist mindset. And, in order to escape from either utopianism or realism, the option of reflexive thought needs to be explored. The essential clash we face in today's world is a collision of mindsets that is more fundamental than rifts between cultures, ethnic backgrounds, or religions. This is the clash between the absolutist mind and the reflexive mind.

ABSOLUTISM VERSUS REFLEXIVITY

The absolutist mindset operates with such notions as the absolute truth and absolute certainty. It aspires toward solid foundations and fixed grounds, and it believes that there needs to be indubitable knowledge or else the world would be hopelessly lost. The absolutist way of thinking has ignored that Immanuel Kant liberated the human mind for speculative exploration, and it falls back on the Cartesian craving for certain knowledge. In morality, the absolutist mind operates with a sharp dichotomy between good and evil: It perceives of evil as "absolute evil." A characteristic of absolutist political talk is that reasoned argumentation is usually absent. In politics, absolutist proposals—even calls to war—lack well-balanced justification and do not invite questioning. The absolutist "either/or" claim is not open to examination, and its sharp dichotomy of good guys versus bad guys hinders the insight that both parties may be wrong. As such, it hampers one's ability to understand a complex and uncertain world. The absolutist mind leaves no space for reflection on the certainty of its own convictions.

Contemporary absolutist speech is a response to what Habermas has described as the "Neue Unübersichtlichkeit": Afraid to lose their grip on reality, people seek certainties and anchorage in a chaotic modern world. The absolutist mindset has not only religious manifestations but also social and political expressions. One finds eco-absolutists that let the protection of the environment prevail without any qualification over all other interests. There are also market-absolutists who believe (at least before the global credit crisis) that we can trust the market blindly. Neoliberal absolutists bestowed the market with divine characteristics: ubiquitous, all-powerful, and all-wise. Absolutist speech can also be observed in advertising, in the "Ad-Speak" of the omnipresent outdoor billboards and commercial TV messages. Their texts proclaim "this is it," and critical reflection is, therefore, not needed. Your salvation is best trusted to the good hands of the "new Gods" of the twenty-first century: the "brands." You cannot live without them. If you ignore them, you are utterly helpless!

Conversely, the reflexive mindset proposes that all claims to validity—be they political, moral, or religious—are open to examination and critique. Reflexive minds are willing to test all ideas in public, listen to those who criticize them, and be open to the need to revise earlier convictions. The core of the reflexive mindset is the urge to ask questions. Reflexive pedagogy as is practiced, for example, in the tradition of Reggio Emilia (see chapter 4) leaves space for questions and uncertainties. That today cosmologists are willing to accept that 96% of the universe consists of invisible dark energy and dark matter that we do not understand and cannot explain is very promising for scientific development. In the same vein, it is an important step that advanced genetics research looks at itself as primarily "driven by ignorance."

Reflexivity can guide the way out of the unproductive dichotomy between utopianism and realism. Utopianism without realism leads to romanticizing about the innate goodness of human beings; however, realism without idealism leads to a nihilism where nothing makes a difference and change is a useless concept.

Reflexivity creates the space and the power for people to change. It does not make people helpless if things do not work out. It does not impose nonachievable aspirations. Instead, it makes people discover how important small steps can be. Reflexivity enables people to think within the inevitable paradoxes of life. It fosters the capacity to accept that mutually exclusive elements can be interrelated.

Most important of all, the reflexive mind opens up to "Sisyphism."

SISYPHISM

Can we overcome evil? No! Although humans may not be inherently evil, the destruction of human dignity is a real-life human possibility. It is a part of who humans are: an imperfect, uncertain, threatened, and vulnerable species.

Can we let evil escalate? Yes! This has happened throughout history and media, in various forms and formats—from ancient mythical scripts and religious narratives, to contemporary hate speech on the Web—all playing an important role in facilitating the spiral of escalation.

Can we tame evil? Yes! This needs reflexivity, acceptance of para-doxes, liberation from utopian visions, a communicative management of public spaces, an early warning before incitement leads to destruction, and learning de-escalatory communications. Within this transformed societal context, the mass media could be useful allies in preventing conflict escalation.

In the moral claim to peaceful life, human moral capacity will often be deficient, and moments of moral balance represent probably our most realistic aspirations. Like other aspirations, the taming of evil is a cultural construct that permanently collides with basic inclinations of human nature and, thus, remains permanently vulnerable to failure.

Human beings are, genetically, a mixture of two great apes: chimpanzees and bonobos. Chimps represent the aggressive and violent features of humanity, whereas bonobos represent humanity's empathic and erotic characteristics (De Waal, 2005).

However, recent research by primatologists has found that the bonobos may, after all, not be such peaceful monkeys and may collectively chase after smaller monkeys to kill and eat them. The findings, reported in *Current Biology* (Suhrbeck & Hohmann, 2008), ruin a pleasant dream. They inform us that even our better genetic partner is not perfect, which reinforces the connection between humanity and inhumanity. However, the new insights do not discharge us from the responsibility to—in the spirit of temporality—realize more bonobo moments and tame our inner chimps!

The discovery that even the emphatic, sex-loving bonobo eats smaller fellow apes is characteristic of Sisyphism. Sisyphus is punished by the Gods for his "scorn of the gods, his hatred of death, and his passion for life" (Camus, 1955, p. 120). His torture consists of pushing a heavy rock up the hill, and when he reaches the summit, the stone comes thundering down. He then goes down and pushes it up—again and again. Sisyphus understands the absurdity of his fate and is able to accept the boundaries within which his life will play out. In a strange way, he can live with the evil of his punishment but also keep rolling because its escalation can be prevented. He creates space for reflection and realizes that the absurd and happiness are inseparable (Camus, 1955, p. 122). As Camus concluded, "One must imagine Sisyphus happy" (p. 123). Camus has taught us that accepting the absurdity of life does not make intense and sense-making life impossible.

FINAL THOUGHTS

The three images at the beginning of this book will continue to haunt humanity. Although the evil they express is part of humanity's history and future, its escalation could have been prevented. As we begin to understand how dispute spirals out of control toward bloody massacre, we can develop tools to tame the inevitable conflict. Humans, the tool-making animals, have a vast talent for producing destructive tools but also an equally impressive capacity to develop tools of reconstruction. Paraphrasing George Bernard Shaw, the essence of humanity is mindfulness toward fellow creatures. This needs the creation of communicative realities that facilitate "agonistic" living: in dispute and disagreement, but not as enemies. If we aspire to this as "utopists," we do indeed contribute to the escalation of conflict. As "realists," we fail to see the human potential for change. Sisyphus teaches us human possibilities and human limitations. He is not blind to the abyss that lies between what humans can and what they actually do. Nonetheless, he does not give up thinking that the gap could be smaller. Sisyphus is neither an incurable romantic nor a conservative cynic. As "Sisyphists," we can accept that even if we realize more "bonobo" moments, the "chimp" always stays with us.

NOTES

‹○›

INTRODUCTION

1. In situations that people experience as humiliating, there is an interaction between the "humiliator" and the "humiliated." There is a school of thought (found, for example, in Stoicism) that proposes that he who does not want to be humiliated cannot be humiliated. The outside world can never cause rational people to feel humiliated. Self-respect is not influenced by others; rather, it represents the value that people recognize in themselves. However, whereas Jesus of Nazareth did not experience his crucifixion as humiliating, this would still not justify the behavior of those who jeered at him and spat on him. Independent of what the inmates of the Abu Ghraib prison experienced, it would seem necessary to condemn the conduct of the wardens as humiliating.

My emphasis is not on the presence or absence of feelings by those who are submitted to humiliating acts. Those feelings are too subjective. My focus is on the perpetrating of acts that can be described as humiliating.

The discourse on violence (in politics, in media, and over coffee tables) tends to focus strongly on the experiences and perceptions of the victims. It is striking how often perpetrators of violence see themselves as victims. They may perceive their violent actions as a response to humiliating acts by others. Violence that is experienced by the victim as senseless can make perfect sense to the perpetrator.

2. For studies on human dignity and humiliation, see www.humiliationstudies .org/.

3. See P. G. Zimbardo (2008).

4. "On December 2, 2002, Rumsfeld authorized the interrogators at Guan-tánamo Bay to use a range of abusive techniques that were already widespread

in Afghanistan, enshrining them as official policy," *International Herald Tribune*, December 19, 2008. As of February 2002, President George W. Bush had signed a memorandum that stated that the Third Geneva Convention did not apply to members of Al-Qaeda or the Taliban. The Convention addresses the treatment of enemy prisoners in wartime (*Time*, January 19, 2009, p. 11).

5. The Peace Treaty of Versailles was signed on June 28, 1919, between the Allied Powers and Germany to formally end world War I. The treaty identified Germany as solely responsible for the war, imposed important military restrictions on Germany, compelled Germany to give up its colonies and several European territories, and ordered Germany to pay a prohibitively large sum in reparations (226 billion Reichsmark, which was later—in 1921—reduced to 132 billion Reichsmark). The treaty created a strong resentment among Germans, who experienced the impositions on Germany as humiliating. This widespread feeling was exploited by the national socialists, who labeled the democratic politicians who had approved the Treaty as "traitors."

CHAPTER 1

1. Following the extensive book on emotions written by Nico Frijda (2005), I use the concept in a functional sense. By and large, emotions serve human purposes fairly well: they modulate and instigate human behavior in accordance with important events (p. 494).

2. I chose the concept "anxiety" because it functions very adequately as a container notion that brings together emotions such as fear, grief, and anger. Moreover, W. H. Auden's *The Age of Anxiety* was an important source of inspiration for thinking about contemporary reality. In addition, in literary works that were important to my research (among them the writings of Camus, Kafka, and Hesse), anxiety is an essential existential experience.

3. The Eurobarometer began in 1973 as a research project of the European Commission. Through interviews, data are collected about the attitudes of European citizens regarding the European Union and about general social and political attitudes of European citizens.

4. The father of Nazi eugenics was psychiatrist Alfred Ploetz, who published in 1895 "The Fitness of Our Race and the Protection of the Weak." His theories about racial cleansing were taught in over twenty German universities by 1932.

5. The Milgram experiment is one of the most well-known experiments in social psychology. Stanley Milgram designed the experiment in 1961 to explore how Adolf Eichmann (the trial for this war criminal took place in 1961) and millions of others had just been following orders when committing mass murder. The experiment measures how willingly people obey orders given by an authority. Milgram wrote about the findings in his book *Obedience to Authority: An Experimental View* (1969).

In his *Harper's* magazine article on "The Perils of Obedience" (1974), Milgram concluded that "Ordinary people, simply doing their jobs, and without any particular hostility on their part, can become agents in a terrible destructive process. Moreover, even when the destructive effects of their work become patently clear, and they are asked to carry out actions incompatible with fundamental standards of morality, relatively few people have the resources needed to resist authority."

Among the theoretical explanations offered by Milgram, there are pertinent implications to explain the spiral of escalation. There is the tendency—especially in situations of crisis—to leave one's group to decide on a course of action, which alleviates one's sense of individual responsibility and supports the leader's belief that he knows what he is doing.

CHAPTER 2

1. The literature on media and violence that was surveyed includes: Anderson & Bushman (2001); Anderson & Bushman (2002, March 29); Bergenfield (1994); Dill & Dill (1998); Donnerstein & Linz (1995); Freedman (2002); Griffiths (1999); Huesmann & Miller (1994); Kirsh (2003); Kirsh (2006); Savage (2004); Schramm, Lyle, & Parker (1961); Strasburger (1995); and Wood, Wong, & Chachere (1991).

2. Apart from inadequate diagnostics, the drugs prescribed by doctors are often not adequately tested and may receive the approval of institutions like the U.S. Food and Drug Administration after clinical trials that were much too short in duration to obtain scientifically valid outcomes. Around the world, millions of badly tested drugs are prescribed daily on the basis of unscientific diagnoses and with little or no knowledge about their effects. Although in media discussions about these drugs (and in the drugs' advertisements) there may be references to their side effects and there may even be warnings issued, the notion of side effects is misleading: People need to first know the effects of the drugs they take!

3. The media tend to give prominence to those voices that represent "cultural essentialism." An important example is the international media space given to Ayaan Hirsi Ali, a controversial critic of Islam, former MP in the Netherlands, and, in 2005, on *Time*'s list of the "100 People Who Shape Our Lives."

4. September 1938 (www.ess.uwe.ac.uk/genocide/Streicher2.htm).

5. "What sort of things do you remember best?" Alice ventured to ask.
"Oh, things that happened the week after next," the Queen replied in a careless tone. (Carroll, 1988, p. 254)

CHAPTER 3

1. The UNESCO Constitution, adopted on November 16, 1945, in London by the General Conference of UNESCO member states, states in its preamble, "That since war begins in the minds of men, it is in the minds of men that the defenses of peace must be constructed."

2. Dr. Theo van Boven is emeritus professor of International Law at the University of Maastricht. He is the former director of the UN Centre for Human Rights in Geneva. On December 16, 2005, the General Assembly of the United Nations adopted the "Basic Principles on the Right to a Remedy and Reparation for Victims of Gross Violations of International Human Rights Law and Serious Violations of International Humanitarian Law." These principles were proposed by Theo van Boven and Cherif Bassiouni.

The Statute of the International Criminal Court (the Hague) also recognizes compensation for victims of gross violations of human rights.

3. Students involved in this seminar came from the Netherlands, the Republic of Surinam, Germany, and Aruba.

4. In a 1917 speech.

CHAPTER 4

1. From a seminar (in Fall 2008) on escalatory versus de-escalatory communication with students at the Zeppelin University in Friedrichshafen, Germany.

2. On November 20, 1989, the UN General Assembly (in resolution 44/25) adopted unanimously the Convention on the Rights of the Child. With this convention, children became—in their own right—subjects of international law.

Although the League of Nations in 1924 and the United Nations in 1959 had issued declarations on the rights of the child, some UN member states felt that these rights should be brought under the authority of binding international law. The convention has been ratified by all UN member states, excepting the United States and Somalia.

Article 13 of the convention provides:

1. The child shall have the right to freedom of expression; this right shall include freedom to seek, receive and impart information and ideas of all kinds, regardless of frontiers, either orally, in writing or in print, in the form of art, or through any other media of the child's choice.
2. The exercise of this right may be subject to certain restrictions, but these shall only be such as are provided by law and are necessary:
    (a) For respect of the rights or reputations of others; or
    (b) For the protection of national security or of public order, or of public health or morals.

In the child-friendly version that was produced by UNICEF, Canada, Article 13 reads, "You have the right to find out things and share what you think with others, by talking, drawing, writing or in any other way unless it harms or offends other people."

3. On the tenth anniversary of the convention in 1999, the Norwegian government and United Nations Children's Fund, UNICEF, organized a meeting at which children, young people, media professionals, and child rights experts discussed the development of children's rights in relation to media. From this meeting emerged the Oslo Challenge. The text of the Oslo Challenge calls on governments, media professionals, media owners, children, and parents to help realize children's rights as laid down in the Convention.

4. Illustrative examples can also be found on the following Web sites: http://www.listenup.org—a youth media network that connects young video producers; http://pbskids.org/dontbuyit—a media literacy site for young people; and http://www.kqed.org/topics/education/medialiteracy/youthmedia—a site that wants to add youth voices to mainstream media. In addition, the Adobe Youth Voices initiative empowers youth worldwide to use multimedia and digital tools to communicate and share ideas; for more info, e-mail youthvoices@adobe.com. The World Radio Forum aims to develop children's and youth radio. Among its goals is that children have the right to participate in radio production. The forum works with children and youth to publish and promote the Radio Manifesto and can be found at http://www

.worldradioforum.org. The Radio Manifesto (the result of three years of discussions with children, launched at the Fourth World Summit on Media & Children, Rio de Janeiro, 2004) can be found at http://www.worldradioforum.org/icyrmanifesto .shtml.

5. For information about Reggio Emilia: http://zerosei.comune.re.it/. On the hundred languages, see Edward, Gandini, & Forman (1998).

6. After a concert in the Amsterdam Bimhuis in 2007 with tenor saxophonist Joe Lovano, many years his junior (from personal conversation with author).

7. See www.rhythmisit.com.

8. According to the report "An Appraisal of the Technologies of Political Control" (Omega Foundation, 1998) the U.S. National Security Agency (NSA) uses intelligence search agents to monitor the communications traffic of European politicians and citizens. The British research bureau Omega found that the U.S. espionage computer network "Echelon" detects keywords in military and political information as well as in economic information used by commercial firms and stores relevant data for later analysis. For a long time, there had been indications of eavesdropping on world communication networks by the NSA, and the Omega report now provided the evidence. The British-American surveillance program targets all the Intelsat satellites that carry the major portion of worldwide telephone calls, fax communications, and Internet traffic. The NSA's main justification for this is the struggle against terrorism and crime. There is, however, little hard evidence that there are indeed positive law enforcement effects. In the meantime, European Parliament members were informed that the NSA routinely intercepts valuable private commercial data about investments, tenders, and mergers.

Interestingly enough, in early 1999 a working group of the European Parliament proposed the establishment of an extensive network to tap into information traffic among citizens and companies. According to the working group, the permanent surveillance of all data traffic in real time is a "must" for law enforcement purposes. In May 1999 the European Parliament resolved to approve the establishment of a comprehensive surveillance system for all European telecommunications traffic on mobile phones, faxes, pagers, and the Internet. The electronic system that is being designed for this massive interception program will track data on phone numbers, e-mail addresses, credit card details, PIN codes, and passwords. Also in 1999 a report on Interception Capabilities informed the European Parliament about the planning by the NSA, the FBI, and the European Union—through the International Law Enforcement Telecommunication Seminar—of a vast surveillance network that would combine national security and law enforcement activities (Hamelink, 2000, pp. 126–127).

CHAPTER 5

1. The importance of the "communicative city" (a concept initiated by the author of this book) can be promoted by an annual award given to a city that, according to the judgment of an international jury with renowned urban designers, planners, architects, urban sociologists, and communication experts, offers optimal opportunities and stimuli for people to engage in disarming conversation.

The award event could be combined with an academic symposium on urbanism and communicative lifestyles. The symposium should stimulate empirical research on the de-escalating potential of urban conversation. Worldwide publicity, through magazine covers, editorials, articles, television news, documentaries, and Internet sites, would help to render the communicative dimension of urban life a core political and sociocultural issue. Through a very attractive and easily accessible Web site, the largest possible number of worldwide urbanites and city visitors should be invited to share their communicative experiences through stories and images. The "communicative city" annual award should be a cooperative project involving such organizations as the United Cities and Local Governments organization, sometimes referred to as the United Nations of Cities, which was launched in May 2004; see www.cities-localgovernments.org.

A second global award could be developed for young urban planners and city architects to honor best design practices for the building of future communicative cities. An interesting option here would be to use the popular SimCity Societies computer game, which enables players to design their own city. The existing game makes it possible to combine six different social energies: productivity, affluence, authority, knowledge, spirituality, and creativity. The nature of the city that players build is defined by combining these energies in different ways. It would be possible to add to these variables the energy of disarming conversation and design a city that offers the conditions for its realization.

2.   The charter was elaborated at the Social Forum of the Americas (Quito, Ecuador, July 2004), the World Urban Forum (Barcelona, Spain, October 2004), and the World Social Forum (Porto Alegre, Brazil, January 2005).

3.   People easily converse with each other in one of the happiest cities in the world (according to the judgment of its citizens), Ringkøbing in Denmark, because people experience trust and security. For data from the happiness project, directed by Ruut Veenhoven, at Erasmus University in Rotterdam, see http://worlddatabaseofhappiness .eur.nl.

4.   Although the theory needs further development and empirical investigation and is often criticized by mainstream psychologists for its theory-research gap, it can be a helpful tool to help understand the obstacles to and opportunities for a dialogical communicative mode. This is important because, by and large, in the various social and behavioral sciences (including communication science), the dialogue has been a neglected domain.

5.   It would seem to me, as an inhabitant of Amsterdam, that this city combines the "hostile city" with the "warm city" in a balance that is very precarious. Problems around issues of incitement to ethnic hatred and concerns about Islamicization could easily tip the balance, leading to a very dangerous zone. This would be very unfortunate for a city that is nicknamed "Mokum" after the Hebrew word *Maqum,* which means the place where everyone can go and feel welcome.

CHAPTER 6

1.   Data on ethnic/religious conflict can be found at the Web site of the Minorities at Risk project: www.cidcm.umd.edu/inscr/mar.

For failed states and domestic violent conflict, a useful source is http://globalpolicy .gmu.edu/pitf.

2. See www.worldwatch.org.

3. Data from International Crime Victim Surveys, see www.unicri.it.

4. The report can be downloaded from www.environmentaldefense.org/ documents/3566-AbruptClimateChange.pdf.

5. Howard (2009) has suggested that such strategies played a role in the 1990 Kuwait-Iraq dispute.

6. Wendy Barnaby is editor of the British Science Association magazine *People & Science*.

7. I borrow—inevitably—the term "imagined" from Benedict Anderson, in which the nation-state is an imagined community (1983).

8. The democratic Weimar Republic (officially known as Deutsches Reich) could not stop an increasingly violent Nazi party from emerging, and, in fact, created the political (the Weimar Constitution made a presidential dictatorship possible, giving the president all the power to act if public order and security were endangered), social (Germans felt a great deal of resentment after the Treaty of Versailles), and economic (there were devastating economic problems—massive unemployment and hyperinflation) conditions for national and, eventually, international armed conflict.

CHAPTER 7

1. The alert system would operate on local and international levels. At the local level, in conflict areas small teams of researchers/analysts would monitor media (newspapers, broadcast media) by analyzing text and images in order to identify contents that incite violence and genocide. Local teams, who could possibly be hosted by UN offices and should cooperate with local academic institutions, human rights groups, and media professionals, would produce regular reports of findings.

At the international level, a clearinghouse would collect local reports and transmit reports and commentaries to the international press, UN agencies, and, whenever appropriate, to the International Criminal Court in the Hague.

2. For more on the responsibility to protect, see http://www.responsibility toprotect.org.

3. The trial chamber issued the following sentences.

Having found the three Accused guilty, the Chamber now proceeds to the sentencing of the Accused.

Ferdinand Nahimana

I call on Ferdinand Nahimana to rise for sentencing and face the Court.

Ferdinand Nahimana, you were a renowned academic, Professor of History at the National University of Rwanda. You were Director of ORINFOR and founded RTLM radio station as an independent private radio. You were Political Adviser to the Interim Government sworn in after 6 April 1994 under President Sindikubwabo. You were fully aware of the power of words, and you used the radio—the medium of communication with the widest public reach—to disseminate hatred and violence. You may have been motivated by your sense of patriotism and the need you perceived for equity for the Hutu population in Rwanda. But instead of following legitimate avenues of recourse, you chose a path of genocide. In doing so, you betrayed the trust placed in you as an intellectual and a leader. Without a firearm, machete or any physical weapon, you caused the deaths of thousands of innocent civilians. Representations were made by your witnesses as to your good character and high standing in society but in the Chamber's view, these circumstances are not mitigating. They underscore your betrayal of public trust. Having considered all the relevant factors, the Chamber sentences you in respect of all the counts on which you have been convicted to imprisonment for the remainder of your life.

Hassan Ngeze

I call on Hassan Ngeze to rise for sentencing and face the Court.

Hassan Ngeze, as the owner and editor of a well-known newspaper in Rwanda, you were in a position to inform the public and shape public opinion toward achieving democracy and peace for all Rwandans. Instead of using the media to promote human rights, you used it to attack and destroy human rights. You had significant media networking skills and attracted support earlier in your career from international human rights organizations who perceived your commitment to freedom of expression. However, you did not respect the responsibility that comes with that freedom. You abused the trust of the public by using your newspaper to instigate genocide. The Chamber notes that you saved Tutsi civilians from death by transporting them across the border out of Rwanda. Your power to save was more than matched by your power to kill. You poisoned the minds of your readers, and by words and deeds caused the death of thousands of innocent civilians.

Having considered all the relevant factors, the Chamber sentences you in respect of all the counts on which you have been convicted to imprisonment for the remainder of your life.

Jean-Bosco Barayagwiza [note from the author: he did not attend the trial because he had no confidence in the chamber] was Director of Political Affairs in the Ministry of Foreign Affairs and a founder of RTLM. He was also the founder of CDR and its President in Gisenyi Prefecture, later National President of CDR. He is a lawyer by training and in his book professes a commitment to international human rights standards. Yet he deviated from these standards and violated the most fundamental human right, the right to life. He did so both through the institutions he created, and through his own personal acts of participation in the genocide. He was the lynchpin of the conspiracy, collaborating closely with both Nahimana and Ngeze.

Having considered all the relevant factors, the Chamber considers that the appropriate sentence for Jean-Bosco Barayagwiza in respect of all the counts on which he has been convicted is imprisonment for the remainder of his life.

However, in its decision dated 31 March 2000, the Appeals Chamber decided:

[T]hat for the violation of his rights the Appellant is entitled to a remedy, to be fixed at the time of judgement at first instance, as follows:

If the Appellant is found not guilty, he shall receive financial compensation;

If the Appellant is found guilty, his sentence shall be reduced to take account of the violation of his rights.

The Chamber considers that a term of years, being by its nature a reduced sentence from that of life imprisonment, is the only way in which it can implement the Appeals Chamber decision. Taking into account the violation of his rights, the Chamber sentences Barayagwiza in respect of all the counts on which he has been convicted to 35 years' imprisonment. Pursuant to Rule 101(D) of the Rules, Barayagwiza is further entitled to credit for time served, to be calculated from the date of his initial arrest in Cameroon, on 26 March 1996. Credit for time served has been calculated as seven years, eight months and nine days. Therefore, Barayagwiza will serve twenty-seven years, three months and twenty-one days, being the remainder of his sentence, as of 3 December 2003.

Pursuant to Rules 102 (A) and 103, the three Accused shall remain in the custody of the Tribunal pending transfer to the State where they will serve their sentences.

Source: www.liveunictr.altmansolutions.com.

4. Free speech can be a fundamentalist claim equal to the claim that a text that is considered sacrosanct by some cannot be criticized by others. The collision of fundamentalist claims is not particularly helpful for de-escalating conflicts. If the clashing parties have an interest in de-escalating (which obviously is not always the case!) they will have to find a communicative mode that helps them respect and at the same time transcend their cherished positions. The modality that is described in chapter 4 as mindful communication may offer that transcending potential.

5. The codification of antihatred provisions began in the 1990s in North America and Europe. A major motivation was the equation of hate speech (i.e., expressions of hatred or contempt—again rather different emotions—toward groups on the basis of their religious, cultural, ethnic, or sexual identity) with discrimination.

There are serious conceptual difficulties with legal provisions against hate speech. First, they use the notion of race, which suggests that there are distinct races. However, the notion of race is problematic because there are no distinct races. Using this notion, therefore, perpetuates a questionable perception of humanity. Hating a race means hating humanity.

Second, the suggestion of the relationship between hatred and discrimination is problematic. This language assumes that hating others implies discriminating against others. There is, however, little, if any, scientific evidence for this assumption. We could equally assume a relationship between love and discrimination. Equating hate propaganda with the promotion of racial discrimination cannot be established unequivocally.

6. Source: www.liveunictr.altmansolutions.com.

7. It is also important to consider that in order to address the incitement to hate, the law represents a very blunt instrument. Hate is the extreme form of hostility that people feel when confronted with what they experience as threats, which they fear. Feelings of hate cannot be resolved by rational argument. Just like the person in love, the "hater" is not open to rational argumentation.

Law, however, uses rational arguments and is, therefore, inadequate to deal with the irrationality of hate. Hate is a psychological problem that is shaped and nursed by a lack of capacity for empathy and an inability to articulate fear, distrust, and revulsion of others in communicable ways. Haters are not necessarily criminals, but they are certainly troubled citizens.

8. Article 2 of the Convention on the Prevention and Punishment of the Crime of Genocide, adopted by the UN General Assembly on 9 December 1948.

9. This is particularly interesting as the World Health Organization has identified the "right to health" as being entitled to a complete state of physical, mental, and social well-being. Therefore, words and images that negatively affect this state are violations of a fundamental human right.

CHAPTER 8

1. Albert Camus (1913–1960), French journalist and philosopher, received in 1957 the Nobel Prize for Literature. He developed in several of his works the paradox of the absurdity of human life: Our lives are ultimately meaningless, which renders the possibility of suicide the only real philosophical question. Yet, we can decide not to kill ourselves! We can even create meaning by our own decisions—for example, through the choice to protect of human rights.

2. *Groundhog Day* is a comedic film released in 1993. It is a story about a TV weatherman (played by Bill Murray) who covers the annual Goundhog Day festival and finds himself in a time loop that makes him repeat the same day over and over again.

3. See also Herfried Münkler, Kant's "perpetual peace": Utopia or political guide? On http://www.opendemocracy.net; posted December 28, 2008.

REFERENCES

༄

Abrahamian, E. (2003). The U.S. media, Huntington and September 11. *Third World Quarterly, 24*(3), 529–544.

Altheide, D. L. (2002). *Creating fear: News and the construction of crisis.* New York: Aldine de Gruyter.

Anderson, C. A., & Bushman, B. J. (2001). Effects of violent video games on aggressive behavior, aggressive cognition, aggressive affect, physiological arousal, and prosocial behavior: A meta-analytic review of the scientific literature. *Psychological Science, 12,* 353–359.

Anderson, C. A., & Bushman, B. J. (2002, March 29). The effects of media violence. *Science, 295,* 2377–2379.

Anderson, B. (1983). *Imagined communities: Reflections on the origin and spread of nationalism.* London/New York: Verso.

Apel, K. O. (1988). *Diskurs und Verantwortung.* Frankfurt: Suhrkamp.

Argyle, M., & Furnham, A. (1983). Sources of satisfaction and conflict in long-term relationships. *Journal of Marriage and the Family, 17,* 278–288.

Ayotte, K. J., & Moore, S. D. (2008). Terrorism, language, and community dialogue. In H. D. O'Hair, R. L. Heath, K. J. Ayotte & G. R. Ledlow (Eds.), *Terrorism: Communication and rhetorical perspectives* (pp. 67–92). Cresskill, NJ: Hampton Press.

Barber, B. R. (2004). *Fear's empire: War, terrorism, and democracy.* New York: W. W. Norton and Company.

Barnaby, W. (2009, March 19). Do nations go to war over water? *Nature, 458*(7236), 282–283.

Baumeister, R. F. (1997). *Evil: Inside human violence and cruelty.* New York: A. W. H. Freeman.

BBC. (2008). Policy Briefing #1. The Kenyan 2007 elections and their aftermath: The role of media and communication. London: BBC World Service Trust.

References

Beck, U. (2002). The cosmopolitan society and its enemies. *Theory, Culture & Society, 19*, 1–2.

Behnke, A. (2008). 'Eternal Peace' as the graveyard of the political: A critique of Kant's Zum Ewigen Frieden. *Millennium—Journal of International Studies, 5*(36), 513–531.

Benesch, S. (2004). Inciting genocide, pleading free speech. *World Policy Journal, 21*(2), 62–69.

Bergenfield, M. (1994). Thirty years of research have proved that exposure to TV violence is hazardous to children's health and welfare. *Parents, 69*(10), 40–45.

Bernstein, R. J. (2005). *The abuse of evil: The corruption of politics and religion since 9/11.* Cambridge, UK: Polity Press.

Boone, M. (2002). Urban space and political conflict in Late-Medieval Flanders. *Journal of Interdisciplinary History, 32,* 621–640.

Boulding, K. E. (1962). *Conflict and defense: A general theory.* New York: Harper.

Boulding, K. E. (1990). *Three faces of power.* London: Sage.

Bourdieu, P. (1984). *Distinction: A social critique of the judgement of taste.* Cambridge, MA: Harvard University Press.

Brown, L. (2008). Draining our future: The growing shortage of freshwater. *The Futurist, 42*(3), 16–22.

Buss, D. M. (2009). *Evolutionary psychology.* Boston: Pearson Education, Inc.

Camus, A. (1955). *The myth of Sisyphus.* New York: Alfred A. Knopf.

Canary, D. J., Cupach, W. R., & Messman, S. J. (1995). *Relationship conflict: Conflict in parent-child, friendship, and romantic relationships.* Thousand Oaks, CA: Sage Publications.

Carhart, T. (2002). *The piano shop on the Left Bank.* New York: Random House.

Carroll, L. (1988). *Alice in wonderland: Through the looking glass.* Harmondsworth, UK: Penguin.

Castells, M. (1991). *The informational city: Information technology, economic restructuring, and the urban-regional process.* Oxford: Blackwell.

Cesari, J. (2005). Mosque conflicts in European cities. *Journal of Ethnic and Migration Studies, 31*(6), 1015–1024.

Chalk, F., & Jonassohn, K. (1990). *The history and sociology of genocide.* New Haven, CT: Yale University Press.

Chang, I. (1997). *The rape of Nanking.* New York: Penguin.

Charter of the International Military Tribunal at Nuremberg. (1945). London.

Cissna, K. N., & Anderson, R. (1998). Theorizing about dialogic moments: The Buber-Rogers position and postmodern themes. *Communication Theory, 8*(1), 63–104.

Citizen's Commission on Human Rights. (2006). *Psychiatry: An industry of death.* Los Angeles, CA: CCHR.

Clarke, E. J., Preston, M., Raskin, J., & Bengtson, V. L. (1999). Types of conflicts and tensions between older parents and adult children. *The Gerontologist, 39,* 261–270.

Cloud, D. (2008). Flying while Arab. In H. D. O'Hair, R. L. Heath, K. J. Ayotte & G. R. Ledlow (Eds.), *Terrorism: Communication and rhetorical perspectives* (pp. 219–236). Cresskill, NJ: Hampton Press.

Connolly, W. E. (1991). *Identity difference: Democratic negotiations of political paradox.* Ithaca, NY: Cornell University Press.

Cosmides, L., & Tooby, J. (1997). Evolutionary psychology: A primer. Retrieved from www.psych.ucsb.edu/research/cep/primer.html.

References

Cottle, S. (2006). *Mediatized conflict: Developments in media and conflict issues.* Maidenhead, Berkshire, UK; New York: Open University Press.

Dahrendorf, R. (2002, May). Getrennt, aber gleichberechtigt. *Der Standard,* p. 39.

Davis, M. (1992). Fortress Los Angeles: The militarization of urban space. In M. Sorkin (Ed.), *Variations on a theme park: Scenes from the new American city and the end of public space* (pp. 154–180). New York: Hill and Wang.

de Waal, F. (2005). *De aap in ons (Our inner ape).* Amsterdam: Contact.

Die Klima-katastrophe. (1986). *Der Spiegel, 33,* cover page, 122.

Dill, K. E., & Dill, J. C. (1998). Video game violence: A review of the empirical literature. *Aggression and Violent Behavior, 3*(4), 407–428.

Donnerstein, E., & Linz, D. (1995). The media. In J. Q. Wilson & J. Petersilia (Eds.), *Crime* (pp. 237–266). San Francisco, CA: Institute for Contemporary Studies Press.

Dorfman, A. (2003, September 29). Lessons of a catastrophe. *The Nation.*

Edward, C., Gandini, L., & Forman, G. (Eds.). (1998). *Hundred languages of children.* London: Ablex Publishing Corporation.

Elias, N. (1982). *The civilizing process: State formation and civilization.* Oxford: Basil Blackwell Publishing.

Elliott, M. (2008, January 17). A tale of three cities. *Time.* Retrieved from www.time.com/time/magazine/article/0,9171,1704398,00.html.

Evans, G. (2008). *The responsibility to protect: Ending mass atrocity crimes for once and for all.* Washington, D.C.: Brookings Institution Press.

Foucault, M. (2003). *Society must be defended: 1975–1976, Lectures at the College de France.* New York: Picador.

Freedman, J. L. (2002). *Media violence and its effect on aggression.* Toronto, Canada: University of Toronto Press.

Friedman, T. L. (2003, November 9). The humiliation factor. *New York Times.*

Freud, S. (1984). *Het onbehagen in de cultuur.* Amsterdam: Boom.

Frijda, N. H. (2005). *De emoties.* Amsterdam: Bert Bakker.

Fromm, E. (1964). *The heart of man: Its genius for good and evil.* New York: Harper & Row.

Furedi, F. (1997). *Culture of fear: Risk-taking and the morality of low expectation.* London: Cassell.

Furedi, F. (2005). *Politics of fear: Beyond left and right.* London: Continuum.

Gallagher, T. (1997). My neighbour, my enemy: The manipulation of ethnic identity and the origins and conduct of war in Yugoslavia. In D. Turton (Ed.), *War and ethnicity: Global connections and local violence* (pp. 47–75). Rochester, NY: The Boydell Press.

Gantzel, K. J. (1997). War in the post-World War II world: Some empirical trends and a theoretical approach. In D. Turton (Ed.), *War and ethnicity: Global connections and local violence* (pp. 123–144). Rochester, NY: The Boydell Press.

Germer, C. K., Siegel, R. D., & Fulton, P. R. (Eds.). (2005). *Mindfulness and psychotherapy.* New York: The Guilford Press.

Giddens, A. (1994). *Beyond left and right: The future of radical politics.* Stanford, CA: Stanford University Press.

Gilkey, L. B. (2001). *On Niebuhr: A theological study.* Chicago: University of Chicago Press.

Goffman, E. (1963). *Behavior in public places: Notes on the social organization of gatherings.* New York: The Free Press.

References

Goldhagen, D. (1997). *Hitler's willing executioners: Ordinary Germans and the Holocaust.* New York: Knopf.

Graham, S. (Ed.). (2004). *Cities, war, and terrorism: Towards an urban geopolitics.* Oxford: Blackwell Publishing.

Graham, S. (2006). The urbanization of political violence. In *UN-Habitat State of the World's Cities* (pp. 150–151). London: Earthscan.

Gray, J. (2007). *Black mass: Apocalyptic religion and the death of utopia.* London: Penguin Group.

Griffiths, M. (1999). Violent video games and aggression: A review of the literature. *Aggression and Violent Behavior, 4*(2), 203–212.

Grossman, D. (1995). *On killing: The psychological cost of learning to kill in war and society.* New York: Little, Brown and Company.

Grupp, S. (2003). Political implications of a discourse of fear: The mass mediated discourse of fear in the aftermath of 9/11. Unpublished paper, Berlin.

Habermas, J. (1993). *Moral consciousness and communicative action.* Cambridge, MA: MIT Press.

Hackett, R. A., & Schroeder, B. (2008). Does anybody practice peace journalism? A cross-national comparison of press coverage of the Afghanistan and Israeli-Hezbollah wars. *Peace & Policy, 13,* 26–61.

Hamelink, C. J. (2000). *The ethics of cyberspace.* London: Sage.

Hamelink, C. J., & Linné, O. (1994). *Mass communication research: On problems and policies.* Norwood, NJ: Ablex Publishing.

Hannikainen, L. (1988). *Peremptory norms in international law.* Helsinki: Finnish Lawyers' Publishing Company.

Harff, B., & Gurr, T. R. (2004). *Ethnic conflict in world politics.* Boulder, CO: Westview Press.

Hermans, H. J. M., Kempen, H. J. G., & van Loon, R. J. P. (1992). The dialogical self: Beyond individualism and rationalism. *American Psychologist,* (47), 23–33.

Heschel, A. J. (1958). Presentation religion in a free society. In *The insecurity of freedom: Essays on human existence* (p. 17) New York: Noonday Press.

Hewitt, J. J., Wilkenfeld, J., & Gurr, T. R. (2008). *Peace and conflict, 2008.* Boulder, CO: Paradigm Publishers.

Hewitt, J. J., Wilkenfeld, J., & Gurr, T. R. (2010). *Peace and conflict, 2010.* Boulder, CO: Paradigm Publishers.

Holl, W. (1985). Geschichtsbewusstsein und Oral History. Geschichtsdidaktische Ueberlegungen. In L. Niethammer & W. Trapp (Eds.), *Lebenserfahrung und Kollektives Gedächtnis* (pp. 63–82). Frankfurt: Suhrkamp.

Holmes, R. (1986). *Acts of war: The behavior of men in battle.* New York: The Free Press.

Horney, K. (1945). *Our inner conflicts: A constructive theory of neurosis.* New York: W. W. Norton & Company.

Howard, R. (2009, September/October). Peak oil and strategic resource wars. *Futurist,* p. 18.

Huesmann, L. R., & Miller, L. S. (1994). Long-term effects of repeated exposure to media violence in childhood. In L. R. Huesmann (Ed.), *Aggressive behavior: Current perspectives* (pp. 153–186). New York: Plenum Press.

Huntington, S. (1993). The clash of civilizations? *Foreign Affairs, 72*(3), 22–49.

Huntington, S. (1997). *The clash of civilizations and the remaking of world order.* London: Touchstone Books.

References

Huntington, S. (2002, January 3). Interview in *Newsweek*.

International Energy Agency. (2008). World energy outlook 2008. Paris: International Energy Agency.

IPCC. (2007). The fourth assessment report of the Intergovernmental Panel on Climate Change. Geneva: IPCC.

Irvan, S. (2006). Peace journalism as a normative theory: Premises and obstacles. *Global Media Journal: Mediterranean Edition, 1*(2), 34–39.

Jackson, R. (2005). *Writing the war on terrorism: Language, politics and counter-terrorism.* Manchester, UK: Manchester University Press.

Kahane, A. (2004). *Solving tough problems: An open way of talking, listening, and creating new realities.* San Francisco, CA: Berrett-Koehler Publishers.

Kellow, C. L., & Steeves, H. L. (1998). The role of radio in the Rwandan genocide. *Journal of Communication, 48*(3) 107–128.

Kirsh, S. J. (2003). The effects of violent video games on adolescents: The overlooked influence of development. *Aggression and Violent Behavior, 8,* 377–389.

Kirsh, S. J. (2006). Cartoon violence and aggression in youth. *Aggression and Violent Behavior, 11,* 547–557.

Klare, M. T. (2001). *Resource wars: The new landscape of global conflict.* New York: Henry Holt and Company.

Kleinnijenhuis, J. J. (2008, December 27). Comment in *NRC-Handelsblad.*

Knightley, P. (2000). *The first casuality: The war correspondent as hero and myth-maker from the Krimea to Kosovo.* London: Prion.

Kuhn T. (1962). *The structure of scientific revolutions.* Chicago: University of Chicago Press.

Kunneman, H. (2005). *Voorbij het dikke-ik.* Amsterdam: Uitgeverij SWP.

Lefebvre, H. (1968). *Le droit à la ville.* Paris: Anthropos.

Licklider, R. (1995). The consequences of negotiated settlements in civil wars, 1945–1993. *American Journal of Political Science, 44,* 84–93.

Louw, E. (2005). *The media and political process.* London: Sage.

Margalit, A. (1996). *The decent society.* Cambridge, MA: Harvard University Press.

Mattelart, A. (2008). *La globalisation de la surveillance.* Paris: La Découverture Poche.

May, R. (1977). *The meaning of anxiety.* New York: W. W. Norton & Company.

Merton, R. K. (1968). *Social theory and social structure.* New York: The Free Press.

Milgram, S. (1963, October). A behavioural study of obedience. *Journal of Abnormal Psychology,* (67), 371–378.

Milgram, S. (1969). *Obedience to authority: An experimental view.* New York: Harper & Row.

Milgram, S. (1974, December). The perils of obedience. *Harper's.*

Minsky, M. (1985). *The society of mind.* New York: Simon & Schuster.

More, T. (1984). *Utopia.* Harmondsworth, UK: Penguin.

Morris, E., & Gourevitch, P. (2008). *Standard operating procedure: A war story.* New York: Picador.

Mouffe, C. (2000). *The democratic paradox.* London: Verso.

Müller, T. (2002). *De warme stad: Betrokkenheid bij het publieke domein.* Utrecht: Jan van Arkel.

Niebuhr, R. (1932). *Moral man and immoral society: A study in ethics and politics.* Louisville, KY: John Knox Press.

Omega Foundation (1998). *An appraisal of the technologies of political control.* Manchester, UK: Omega Foundation.

Orians, G. (1980). Habitat selection: General theory and applications to human behavior. In J. S. Lockard (Ed.), *The evolution of human social behaviour* (pp. 49–66). London: Allen & Unwin.

Orians, G. (1986). An ecological and evolutionary approach to landscape aesthetics. In E. C. Penning-Roswell & D. Lowenthal (Eds.), *Landscape meaning and values* (pp. 3–25). New York, Oxford University Press.

Owen, D. (2008). *In sickness and in power: Illness in heads of state during the last 100 years.* London: Methuen Publishing.

Owen, J. (2007, September 7). Syria mass graves suggest ancient urban conflict. *National Geographic.* Retrieved from http://news.nationalgeographic.com/news/2007/09/070907-syria-graves.html.

Perry, A. (2008, November 27). Weather wars. *Time.* Retrieved from http://www.time.com/time/magazine/article/0,9171,1862670,00.html.

Popper, K. R. (1963). *Conjectures and refutations: The growth of scientific knowledge.* London: Routledge.

Power, S. (2002). *A problem from hell: America and the age of genocide.* Basic Books: New York).

Pringle, E. (2009, December 12). Truthout report. Retrieved from www.truth-out.org.

Pruitt, D. G., & Kim, S. H. (2004). *Social conflict: Escalation, stalemate, and settlement.* New York: McGraw-Hill.

Raes, K. (1995). Vrijheid van Meningsuiting en de revisionistische geschiedvervalsing. In G. A. I. Schuyt & D. Voorhoof (Eds.), *Vrijheid van meningsuiting, racisme en revisionisme* (pp. 31–78). Gent: Academia Press.

Roht-Arriaza, N. (1995). *Impunity and human rights in international law and practice.* Oxford: Oxford University Press.

Rosenberg, M. B. (2003). *Non-violent communication.* Encinitas, CA: Puddle Dancer Press.

Rosenblum, M. (1993). *Who stole the news?* New York: John Wiley & Sons.

Rummel, R. J. (1997). *Democide: Genocide and mass murder since 1900.* Charlottesville: University of Virginia.

Sandole, D. J. D. (1984). The subjectivity of theories and actions in world society. In M. Banks (Ed.), *Conflict in world society: A new perspective on international relations* (pp. 39–55). Sussex: Wheatsheaf Books.

Sartre, J. P. (1947). *Huis Clos.* Paris: Gallimard.

Sassen, S. (2001). *The global city: New York, London, Tokyo.* Princeton, NJ: Princeton University Press.

Savage, J. (2004). Does viewing violent media really cause criminal violence? A methodological review. *Aggression and Violent Behavior, 10,* 99–128.

Schattschneider, E. E. (1960). *The semi-sovereign people: A realist's view of democracy in America.* Hinsdale, IL: The Dryden Press.

Schramm, W., Lyle, J., & Parker, E. B. (1961). *Television in the lives of our children: A cross-national comparison.* Stanford, CA: Stanford University Press.

Schramm, W., & Rivers, W. L. (1969). *Responsibility in mass communication.* New York: Harper & Row.

Schwartz, P., & Randall, D. (2003). *An abrupt climate change and its implications for United States national security.* Washington, D.C.: Pentagon.

Sen, A. (2006). *Identity and violence: The illusion of destiny.* New York: W. W. Norton & Company.

References

Senate Armed Services Committee. (2008, December). Inquiry into the treatment of detainees in U.S. custody. http://www.levin.senate.gov/newsroom/supporting/2008/Detainees.121108.pdf.

Shaw, M. (2003). *War and genocide: Organized killing in modern society.* Oxford: Polity Press.

Shinar, D. (2008). Why not more peace journalism? The coverage of the 2006 Lebanon War in Canadian and Israeli media. *Peace & Policy, 13,* 8–25.

Simon, H. A. (1957). *Models of man—social and rational.* New York: John Wiley & Sons.

Smetana, J. G. (1989). Adolescents' and parents' reasoning about actual family conflict. *Child Development,* (60), 1052–1067.

Solomon, L. (2008). *The deniers: The world-renowned scientists who stood up against global warming hysteria, political persecution, and fraud and those who are too fearful to do so.* Minneapolis, MN: Richard Vigilante Books.

Sontag, S. (2002). *Regarding the pain of others.* London: Hamilton.

Sontag, S. (2003, February 1). The Telling Shot. *The Guardian.*

Sorkin, M. (Ed.). (1992). *Variations on a theme park: Scenes from the new American city and the end of public space.* New York: Hill and Wang.

Sprey, J. (1969). The family as a system in conflict. *Journal of Marriage and the Family, 31,* 699–706.

Stearns, P. N. (2006). *American fear: The causes and consequence of high anxiety.* London: Routledge.

Strasburger, V. C. (1995). *Adolescents and the media: Medical and psychological impact.* London: Sage.

Strauss, C. L. (1966). *The savage mind.* Chicago: The University of Chicago Press.

Suhrbeck, M., & Hohmann, G. (2008). Primate hunting by bonobos at Luikotale, Salongo National Park. *Current Biology, 18*(19), 906–907.

Thomas, W. I. (1928). *The child in America: Behavior problems and programs.* New York: Alfred A. Knopf.

Time. (2009, January). Vol. 173(3), p. 13.

Tuchman, B. W. (1979). *A distant mirror: The calamitous 14th century.* New York: Ballantine Books.

Tuchman, B. W. (1984). *The march of folly: From Troy to Vietnam.* New York: Knopf.

UNESCO. (1945). The constitution of UNESCO. London: UNESCO.

United Nations. (1948a). Convention on the prevention and punishment of the crime of genocide. New York: United Nations.

United Nations. (1948b). Universal declaration of human rights. New York: United Nations.

United Nations. (1966a). International convention on the elimination of all forms of racial discrimination. New York: United Nations.

United Nations. (1966b). International covenant on civil and political rights. New York: United Nations.

United Nations. (1989). Convention on the rights of the child. New York: United Nations.

United Nations. (2006). UNDP human development report of 2006. New York: United Nations.

UN-Habitat. (2006). State of the world's cities: Nairobi. UN-Habitat.

UN-Habitat. (2007). Global report on human settlements: Nairobi. UN-Habitat.

United States Armed Services Committee. (2008). Report on treatment of detainees in U.S. Custody. Washington, D.C.: U.S. Senate.

References

van Ginneken, J. (1998). *Understanding global news*. London: Sage.

Volkan, V. (2004). *Blind trust: Large groups and their leaders in times of crisis and terror.* Charlottesville, NC: Pitchstone Publishing.

Waller, J. (2007). *Becoming evil: How ordinary people commit genocide and mass killing.* Oxford: Oxford University Press.

Warren, R. (2004). City streets—The war zones of globalization: Democracy and military operations on urban terrain in the early twenty-first century. In S. Graham (Ed.), *Cities, war and terrorism: Towards an urban geopolitics*. Oxford: Blackwell Publishing.

Wasko, J. (2001). *Understanding Disney: The manufacture of fantasy*. Oxford: Wiley-Blackwell.

Wiesel, E. (1986). The Nobel acceptance speech. Retrieved from www.pbs.org/eliewiesel/nobel/index.html.

Wirth, L. (1938). Urbanism as a way of life. *The American Journal of Sociology, 44*(1), 1–24.

Wood, W., Wong, F., & Chachere, J. G. (1991). Effects of media violence on viewers' aggression in unconstrained social interaction. *Psychological Bulletin, 109*, 371–383.

Wrangham, R., & Peterson, D. (1996). *Demonic males: Apes and the origin of human violence*. Boston: Houghton Mifflin.

Wright-Mills, C. (1956). *The power elite*. Oxford: Oxford University Press.

Zimbardo, P. G. (2006, December 4). Van elk fatsoenlijk mens valt een duivel re maken. Interview in online magazine Elsevier.

Zimbardo, P. G. (2008). *The Lucifer effect: Understanding how good people turn evil*. New York: Random House.

FURTHER READING

∽

Abbott, A. (2004). *Methods of discovery: Heuristics for the social sciences.* New York: Norton.

Achino-Loeb, M-L. (2006). *Silence: The currency of power.* New York: Berghahn Books.

Achterhuis, A. (1998). *De erfenis van de Utopie.* Amsterdam: AMBO.

Alexander, A., Kang, S., & Kim, Y. (2006). Cyberkids. In L. H. Turner & R. West (Eds.), *The family communication sourcebook* (pp. 315–334). London: Sage.

Allen, D. J. (1970). *The philosophy of Aristotle* (2nd ed.). Oxford: Oxford University Press.

Archibugi, A., & Held, D. (Eds). (1995). *Cosmopolitan democracy.* Oxford: Polity Press.

Bambert, J. (2002). *Body of Secrets.* New York: Bantam Books.

Banks, M. (Ed.) (1984) *Conflict in world society.* Sussex: Wheatsheaf Books.

Barber, B. R. (1984). *Strong democracy: Participatory politics for a new age.* Berkeley: University of California Press.

Barge, J. K., & Little, M. (2002). Dialogical wisdom, communicative practice, and organizational life. *Communication Theory, 12*(4), 375–397.

Beck, U. (1992). Risk Society. London: Sage.

Becker, J. (2004). Contributions by media to crisis prevention and conflict settlement. *Conflict and Communication Online, 3*(1/2). Retrieved from www.cco .regenr-online.de.

Bensley, L., & Van Eenwyck, J. (2001). Video games and real-life aggression: Review of the literature. *Journal of Adolescent Health, 29,* 244–257.

Bobbio, N. (1995). Democracy and the international system. In A. Archibugi & D. Held (Eds.), *Cosmopolitan democracy* (pp. 17–41). Oxford: Polity Press.

Bohm, D. (1996). *On dialogue.* London: Routledge.

Boulding, K. E. (1956). *The image: Knowledge in life and society.* Ann Arbor: University of Michigan Press.

Bryant, J. A., & Bryant, J. (2006). Implications of living in a wired family. In L. H. Turner & R. West (Eds.), *The family communication sourcebook* (pp. 297–314). London: Sage.

Burton, J. W. (1969). *Conflict and communication: The use of controlled communication in international relations.* London: MacMillan.

Canetti. E. (2000). *Crowds and power.* London: Phoenix Press.

Carter, A., & Stokes, G. (Eds.). (2002). *Democratic theory today.* Oxford: Polity Press.

Cupach, W. R., & Canary, D. J. (1997). *Competence in interpersonal conflict.* Long Grove, IL: Waveland Press.

de Cauter, L. (2005). *De capsulaire samenleving: Over de stad in het tijdperk van de angst.* Rotterdam: Nai Uitgevers.

Denton, R. E. Jr. (Ed.). (2000). *Political communication ethics: An oxymoron?* London: Praeger.

Deutsch, M. (1973). *The resolution of conflict.* New Haven, CT: Yale University Press.

Dower, N. (1998). *World ethics.* Edinburgh, Scotland: Edinburgh University Press.

Dozier, R. W. (2002). *Why we hate.* New York: McGraw-Hill.

Duchrow, U., & Hinkelammert, F. J. (2004). *Property for people, not for profit.* London: Zed Books.

Dyer, G. (1985). *War.* London: Guild Publishing.

Esser, D. (2004, January). Achieving peace in crisis cities—Reflections on urban conflict transformation and the nation state project. MIT OpenCourseWare. Retrieved from www.ocw.mit/courses.

Etzioni, A. (1993). *The spirit of community: The reinvention of American society.* New York: Touchstone.

Falk, R. (1995). *On humane governance.* Oxford: Polity Press.

Femia, J. V. (1987). *Gramsci's political thought.* Oxford: Clarendon Press.

Freire, P. (1974). *Paedagogik der solidaritaet.* Wuppertal: Hammer Verlag.

Fromm, E. (1973). *The anatomy of human destructiveness.* New York: Holt, Rinehart and Winston.

Galtung, J. (1980). *The true worlds.* New York: The Free Press.

Galtung, J., & Vincent, R. (1992). *Global Glasnost: Towards a new world communication order?* Cresskill: Hampton Press.

Giddens, A. (1991). *Modernity and self-identity: Self and society in the late modern age.* Cambridge, UK: Polity Press.

Gould, C. C. (1988). *Rethinking democracy.* Cambridge: Cambridge University Press.

Gould, C. C. (2004). *Globalizing democracy and human rights.* Cambridge: Cambridge University Press.

Gray, J. (2002). *Straw dogs: Thoughts on humans and other animals.* London: Granta Books.

Gross, B. (1980). *Friendly fascism. The new face of power in America.* New York: M. Evans.

Gurtov, M. (1988). *Global politics in the human interest.* Boulder: Lynne Rienner.

Hackett, R. A., & Zhao, Y. (1998). *Sustaining democracy? Journalism and the politics of objectivity.* Toronto: Garamond Press.

Hallin, D. C., & Mancini, P. (2004). *Comparing media systems.* Cambridge: Cambridge University Press.

Held, D. (1995). *Democracy and the global order.* Cambridge: Cambridge University Press.

Hermans, H. J. M., & Hermans-Konopka, A. (2009). *Dialogical self-theory: Positioning and counterpositioning in a globalizing society.* Cambridge: Cambridge University Press.

Hogg, M. A., & Abrams, D. (Eds). (2001). *Intergroup relations: Essential readings.* Philadelphia: Psychology Press.

Höijer, B. (2004). The discourse of global compassion: The audience and media reporting of human suffering. *Media, Culture & Society, 26*(4), 513–531.

Howard, R. (2005). The media's role in war and peacebuilding. In G. Junne & W. Verkoren (Eds.), *Postconflict development* (pp. 117–128). Boulder, CO: Lynne Rienner.

Ignatieff, M. (2004). *The lesser evil.* Toronto: Penguin Group.

Jacobs, A. B. (1993). *Great streets.* Boston, MIT Press.

James, W. (1909). *A pluralistic universe.* New York: Longmans, Green, and Co.

Jervis, R. (1976). *Perception and misperception in international politics.* Princeton, NJ: Princeton University Press.

Kierulf, A., & Rønning, H. (Eds.). (2009). *Freedom of speech abridged?* Gothenburg, Sweden: University of Gothenburg, Nordicom.

Lederach, J., Paul, J., & Maiese, M. (2003). Conflict transformation. In G. Burgess & H. Burgess (Eds.), *Beyond intractability.* Conflict Research Consortium, University of Colorado, Boulder. Retrieved from www.beyondintractability.org/essay/transformation.

Lee, P. (Ed.). (1995). *The democratization of communication.* Cardiff, UK: University of Wales Press.

Lehrer, K. (1990). *Theory of knowledge.* London: Routledge.

Lipari, L. (2004). Listening for the other: Ethical implications of the Buber-Levinas encounter. In *Communication Theory, 14(2),* pp. 122–141.

Lorenz, K. (1967). *On aggression.* New York: Bantam Books.

Lukes, S. (1974). *Power: A radical view.* London: MacMillan.

Lynch, J., & McGoldrick, A. (2005). *Peace journalism.* Gloucestershire, UK: Hawthorn Press.

Lynch, K. (1960). *The image of the city.* Cambridge, MA: The MIT Press.

MacIver, D. (Ed.). (2004). *Political issues in the world today.* Manchester, UK: Manchester University Press.

MacPherson, C. B. (1962). *The political theory of possessive individualism.* Oxford: Oxford University Press.

Melone, S. D., Terzis, G., & Ozsel, B. (2002).Using the media for conflict transformation: The common ground experience. In *Berghoff Handbook for Conflict Transformation.* Berlin: Berghof Research Center for Constructive Conflict Management. Retrieved from www.berghof.handbook.net/

Miller, L. H. (1990). *Global order: Values and power in international politics.* Boulder, CO: Westview Press.

Monbiot, G. (2003). *The age of consent: A manifesto for a new world order.* London: Flamingo.

Morris, C. W. (1980). Human autonomy and the natural rights to be free. *The Journal of Libertarian Studies, 4*(4), 379–392.

Mueller, C. (1973). *The politics of communication.* Oxford: Oxford University Press.

Muller, U., Goegold, S., & Arhelder, M. (Eds.). (2004). *Gesteuerte demokratie.* Hamburg: VSA Verlag.

Neiman, S. (2004). *Evil in modern thought.* Princeton, NJ: Princeton University Press.

O'Hair, H. D., Heath, R. L., Ayotte, K. J., & Ledlow, G. R. (Eds.). (2008). *Terrorism: Communication and rhetorical perspectives*. Cresskill, NJ: Hampton Press.

Olendzki, A. (2005). The roots of mindfulness. In C. K. Germer, R. D. Siegel & P. R. Fulton (Eds.), *Mindfulness and Psychotherapy* (pp. 241–261). New York: The Guilford Press.

Peeter, J. (2006). *De gekwetste mens*. Budel: Damon.

Pettiford, L. (2004). Democratisation. In D. MacIver (Ed.), *Political issues in the world today* (pp. 33–47). Manchester, UK: Manchester University Press.

Plato. (1974). *The Republic* (Penguin Classic Edition). Harmondsworth, UK: Penguin.

Polk, W. (1997). *Neighbors and strangers: The fundamentals of foreign affairs*. Chicago: University of Chicago Press.

Popper, K. R. (1976). *Unended quest: An intellectual biography*. La Salle, IL: Open Court.

Richardson, L. (2006). *What terrorists want: Understanding the enemy, containing the threat*. New York: Random House.

Roberts, A. (2006). *Blacked out: Government secrecy in the information age*. Cambridge: Cambridge University Press.

Roloff, M. E., & Miller, C. W. (2006). Mulling about family conflict and communication: What we know and what we need to know. In L. H. Turner & R. West (Eds.), *The family communication sourcebook* (pp. 143–164). London: Sage.

Rosenberg, M. (1979). *Conceiving the self*. New York: Basic Books.

Safranski, R. (2003). *Wieviel globalisierung verträgt der Mensch?* Vienna: Carl Hanser Verlag.

Scheff, T. J. (1994). Bloody revenge. Emotions, nationalism and war. Bloomington, IN: iUniverse.com, Inc.

Scheper, E. E. (2005). Preventing deadly conflict in divided societies in Asia: The role of local NGOs. PhD dissertation, Universiteit van Amsterdam.

Seib, P. (2004). *Beyond the front lines: How the news media cover a world shaped by war*. New York: Palgrave MacMillan.

Seidler, V. J. (2007). *Urban fears and global terrors: Citizenship, multicultures and belongings after 7/7*. London: Routledge.

Shafer, J. (2009, April 2). The water-war myth. *Slate*. Retrieved from www.slate.com/id/2215263/

Shalit, B. (1988). *The psychology of conflict and combat*. New York: Praeger Publishers.

Sherif, M. (2001). Superordinate goals in the reduction of intergroup conflict. In M. A. Hogg & D. Abrams (Eds.), *Intergroup relations* (pp. 64–70). Philadephia, PA: Psychology Press.

Shinar, D. (2004). Media peace discourse: Negotiating global media ethics. *Conflict & Communication Online, 3*(1/2).

Shulsky, A. N., & Schmitt, G. J. (2002). *Silent warfare: Understanding the world of intelligence*. Washington, D.C.: Potomac Books.

Siglitz, J. (2002). *Globalisation and its discontents*. London: Penguin Books.

Smith, A. M. (1998). *Laclau and Mouffe: The radical democratic imaginary*. London: Routledge.

Staub, E. (1989). *The roots of evil: The origins of genocide and other group violence*. Cambridge: Cambridge University Press.

Tajfel, H., & Turner, J. (2001). An integrative theory of intergroup conflict. In M. A. Hogg & D. Abrams (Eds.), *Intergroup relations* (pp. 94–109). Philadephia, PA: Psychology Press.

Further Reading

Taylor, P. (1990). *Munitions of the mind: War propaganda from the ancient world to the nuclear age*. Wellingborough, UK: Patrick Stephens, Ltd.

Tumber, H., & Palmer, J. (2004). *Media at war: The Iraq crisis*. London: Sage.

Tumber, H., & Webster, F. (2006). *Journalists under fire: Information war and journalistic practices*. London: Sage.

Turner, L. H., & West, R. (2006). *The family communication sourcebook*. London: Sage.

Turton, D. (Ed.). (1997). *War and ethnicity: Global connections and local violence*. Rochester, NY: The Boydell Press.

UNDP. (2006). *Human development report*. New York: United Nations Development Programme.

UNRISD. (1995). *States of disarray: The social effects of globalization*. Geneva: United Nations Research Institute for Social Development.

Vansielegehem, N. (2006). *Gesprek als grenservaring: Een analyse van Filosoferen met Kinderen als pedagogisch project*. Gent, Belgium: Universiteit Gent.

Varis, T. (Ed.). (1986). *Peace and communication*. San José, Costa Rica: Editorial Universidad para la Paz.

Volkan, V. D. (1998). *The need to have enemies and allies: From clinical practice to international relationships*. London: Jason Aronson, Inc.

Volkan, V. D. (2006). *Killing in the name of identity: A study of bloody conflicts*. Charlottesville, NC: Pitchstone Publishing.

von Bülow, A. (2003). *Die CIA und der 11, September*. München: Piper Verlag.

Walpen, B. (2004). *Die offenen Feinde und ihre Gesellschaft: Eine hegemonietheoretische Studie zur Mont Pèlerin Society*. Hamburg, Germany: VSA Verlag.

Walzer, M. (1983). *Spheres of justice*. Oxford: Blackwell Publishers.

Warner, D. (1991). *An ethic of responsibility in international relations*. Boulder, CO: Lynne Rienner.

Welzer, H. (2008). *Klimakriege*. Frankfurt, Germany: Fischer Verlag.

Wolfsfeld, G. (2004). *Media and the path to peace*. Cambridge: Cambridge University Press.

Woodiwiss, A. (2005). *Human rights*. London: Routledge.

Zakaria, F. (2003). *The future of freedom: Illiberal democracy at home and abroad*. New York: W. W. Norton and Company.

Zelizer, B. (2004). *Taking journalism seriously*. London: Sage.

169

INDEX

heterogeneity, 116; and communicative city, 88–89
Hirsi Ali, Ayaan, 149n3
Hitler, Adolf, 47–48, 141
Holocaust, 26, 126–127. *See also* Nazi Germany; Nuremberg Trials
Houghton, John, 41
human dignity, 6–7, 128
humanitarian intervention, 120
human progress, 138
human relationships, 9–17
human rights, 6–7; and communicative city, 86–88; and freedom of expression, 132–133, 155n4; reparations, 62–63, 149n2. *See also* international human rights law
human scale, 88
humiliation, 2, 4–7, 147n1; acts of, 4–5; and Germany, 7, 148n5
Huntington thesis, 52–54

ICC. *See* International Criminal Court
identity conflict, 114–119; increase in, 116–117; and otherness, 115–116; and religion, 117–119. *See also* conflict
IMT. *See* International Military Tribunal of Nuremberg
inclusiveness, 81
incompatibility, 13
An Inconvenient Truth (documentary), 40
India, 99
individualism, 24
inequality, 58
information, 59–61
information revolution, 137–138
inhumanity, 138
injustice, 19–20
institutions, 5–6
instrumental speech, 76
Intelsat satellites, 151n8
interdependent relationships, 10; and power, 13
Intergovernmental Panel on Climate Change (IPCC), 40–41
intergroup conflict, 94–95; and communication, 58. *See also* conflict
International Convention on the Elimination of All Forms of Racial Discrimination, 127

International Covenant on Civil and Political Rights, 127
International Criminal Court (ICC), 124, 149n2
International Criminal Tribunal for Rwanda, 54, 129–132, 133–134, 153–154n3
international human rights, 6–7. *See also* human rights
international human rights law, 127–132, 133; and prosecution and trial, 128–129. *See also* human rights
international law. *See* international human rights law
International Law Enforcement Telecommunication Seminar, 151n8
International Media Alert System (IMAS), 125, 153n1; and hate speech, 135; and research, 135–136. *See also* early warning system; media
International Military Tribunal of Nuremberg, 129; charter, 123, 124–125
Internet, 67
interrogation, 5–6, 147–148n4
intersubjective space, 58
invisible line, 18
IPCC. *See* Intergovernmental Panel on Climate Change
Iraq, 99, 141
issues, 13

Jaworski, Joseph, 64
Johnson, Hiram, 66
Johnson, Lyndon, 47, 48
Jones, Hank, 80
journalism, 61; and certainty, 33–34; and W questions, 32–33. *See also* media; peace journalism

Kahane, Adam, 63–64
Kangura, 54, 130, 132
Kant, Immanuel, 139, 140, 143
Kaplan, Robert, 53
Karadzic, Radovan, 26
Kennedy, John F., 48
Kenya, 51–52, 125
Khomeiny, Ruhollah, 118
Kleinnijenhuis, Jan, 44

Oedipus, 141–142
oil conflict, 110–111
openness, 88
Oregon Petition Project, 41
Oslo Challenge, 78, 150n3
otherness, 115–116
outdoor activities, 87

Pachauri, Rajendra, 41
parent-child conflict, 11
Patriot Act, 81
peace journalism, 61–62, 65–67; flaws in, 65–66. *See also* journalism; media
Peace of Westphalia, 125
peer review, 56
perception, 13; of injustice, 19–20; of reality, 10–11
personal development, 11
pictures, of warfare, 35
Pires, Maria, 80
Platonic proposition, 79
playgrounds, 88
Ploetz, Alfred, 148n4
polemic speech, 74–75
political leaders: and agitation, 44–48; celebrity status for, 46–47; mental disorders of, 47–48. *See also* leadership
politics, 12–13; and absolutist speech, 72; and anxiety, 24–25
Pol Pot, 15, 47–48, 141
positions, 14
power, 21; and interdependent relationships, 13; and media, 37–38
privatized public space, 87. *See also* public space
prosecution and trial, 128–129
psychopharmaca, 42–43, 149n2
public space: and disarming conversation, 87–88; and mindful communication, 81. *See also* urban space

racial discrimination, 127. *See also* discrimination
Radio Manifesto, 150–151n4
Radio-Télévision Libre des Mille Collines (RTLM), 50, 130, 131–132
Raskovic, Jovan, 26
Rattle, Sir Simon, 80

realism, 142–143
reality, 10–11
reflexive speech, 72
reflexivity: and disarming conversation, 88; vs. absolutism, 143–144
Reggio Emilia project, 79
relational speech, 76
religion; and alienation, 52–54; and group conflict, 99–101; and humiliation, 7; and identity conflict, 117–119; and urban conflict, 107
resource conflict, 109–113; and oil conflict, 110–111; and water conflict, 111–113. *See also* conflict
resources, 106
responsibility to protect, 125
revenge, 19–20
Rice, Condoleezza, 120
right to health, 135, 155n9
Ringkøbing, Denmark, 151n8
ritualizations, 17
Roberts, Pat, 53
Rogers, Carl, 73, 75
Roosevelt, Theodore, 47
RTLM. *See* Radio-Télévision Libre des Mille Collines
Rumsfeld, Donald, 5, 6, 147–148n4
Rushdie, Salman, 53
Rwanda, 49–50; and accusation in a mirror, 54; and crimes against humanity, 129–132, 133–134. *See also* International Criminal Tribunal for Rwanda

Saddam Hussein, 33–34
"satisficing," 8
savanna hypothesis, 89
Schneider, Stephan, 41–42
Schola Cantorum, 80
Schwarzkopf, Norman, 33
science, 12
scientific publication, 56
scientists, 55–56
security, 106
segregation, 108
selective articulation, 32
selective perception, 19
self-determination, 98–99
self-fulfilling prophecy, 141–142

war journalism, 32, 61. *See also* journalism
Washington Post, 53
water conflict, 111–113
Web 2.0, 67
Weimar Republic, 119, 120, 153n8
Wilson, Woodrow, 48
Wohlauf, Vera, 2
Wolfowitz, Paul, 53

World Charter on the Right to the City, 87, 152n2
World Future Society conferences, 56
World Health Organization, 155n9
World Radio Forum, 150–151n4

Youth, 107
Yugoslavia, 133

ABOUT THE AUTHOR

Cees J. Hamelink is Professor of Human Rights and Public Health at the Athena Institute at Vrije Universiteit in Amsterdam and Professor of Management of Information and Knowledge for Sustainable Development at the University of Aruba in Oranjestad, Aruba, as well as Professor Emeritus of International Communication at the University of Amsterdam. He worked as a foreign correspondent for radio and television and was formerly a policy adviser and researcher for several intergovernmental organizations and national governments. He is Editor-in-Chief of the *International Communication Gazette,* is the Honorary President of the International Association for Media and Communication Research, and has authored sixteen books on communication, culture, and human rights.

MEDIA and POWER

David L. Paletz, Series Editor
Duke University